2- 3- 20

To my dear friend, Ray
with love,
        Linda

INTUITION *magic*

Understanding Your Psychic Nature

Other Books by Linda Keen

The Dream Keepers
John Lennon in Heaven

INTUITION
magic

Understanding Your Psychic Nature

LINDA KEEN

Keen Press
CALIFORNIA

The very first edition of this book, *Intuitieve Ontwikkeling* (*Intuitive Development*), was published in the Dutch language in 1985 by Uitgeverij Ankh-Hermes bv, and is now in its 19th printing. The first English edition, *Intuition Magic: Understanding Your Psychic Nature*, was published in 1998 by Hampton Roads Publishing Co., Inc. This is the second English edition of *Intuition Magic*, published 2019 by Keen Press.

Keen Press
www.keenintuition.com

Book Design by Bri Bruce Productions
www.bribruceproductions.com

This book is dedicated to all the teachers and students of the world.

CONTENTS

PART TWO:
INTUITION MAGIC WORKSHOP

The Belly
The Solar Plexus
The Heart
The Throat
The Brow
The Crown
Hands and Feet
Getting to Know Your Chakras
Chakra Color Meditation
Chakra Balancing
Chakra Breathing

INTUITION .
magic

Foreword

How little we know about human consciousness! Many years ago, the mathematician-philosopher Alfred North Whitehead said, "Our minds are finite, and yet even in these circumstances of finitude we are surrounded by possibilities that are infinite, and the purpose of human life is to grasp as much as we can out of that infinitude."(*Dialogues of Alfred North Whitehead*) A friend gave me Whitehead's book to read during a very troubled period when I was searching for answers to experiences I'd had while in a coma, and these words had encouraged me.

During the coma I had the sensation of leaving my body, encountering the *other side*, and then hovering above the hospital room where my body lay. From my vantage point, I barely recognized my own body, withered and emaciated in the bed. It was about three a.m., which I knew because of a clock on the wall. So when I saw my father enter and sit by the bed, I knew something was seriously wrong. He took my hand and began to cry. I had never seen him cry before and I thought it was very peculiar; His grief puzzled me.

I was aware that if I chose to live, I would live. And if I chose to die, I would die. But I failed to find any reason to choose one or the other As I watched my father; however; something happened. I saw that there was a powerful connection between us that caused him to pour out his grief.

What was it? I suppose I had the word for it—love. But that didn't help. What grabbed my attention was the mystery of that invisible bond. What unseen force caused such compelling emotion?

I am certain that it was out of deference to my father; joined with my curiosity about the nature of the bond triggering his grief, that I made the decision to return to my body. In the weeks ahead, I fought to live. I also fought to regain my physical coordination and sight, which I had lost to the burning fever.

I became acutely aware of my body, my mind, and the reality that we can neither see, hear, taste, smell, nor touch. I had awakened to the unseen world that influences our lives profoundly, yet is only rarely acknowledged. Along with these new awarenesses came the recognition of the infinite capacity of human consciousness. Until then I had automatically made certain assumptions about human knowing. I was, after all, a teenager at the time and until then my attention had been much more on my glands than on such obscure metaphysical issues.

For me, that near-death experience stripped away the veils between the physical and spiritual realms. Forty years ago, growing up in rural Michigan, there had been nobody to help me come to terms with what had been awakened in me. For fifteen years thereafter, I searched for answers and found few. Mostly I questioned my own sanity, as I began having experiences I could not explain. I began knowing things that I had never studied or read in books. I began to have precognition and psychic "flashes" in which I would clearly and accurately know a person's thoughts and feelings without them telling me.

While my own search for understanding took a different path from the one Linda Keen so beautifully describes in this book, our destinations are much the same. She has come to a place of knowing and being able to make use of the invisible reality that is the foundation for all our lives.

As you will discover in the pages ahead, embracing the intuitive and spiritual powers of our lives is not always easy. In fact, it can be frightening and even painful at times. The author's skill with words allows us to fully share the experience of emergence, and in the process she prepares us for the path ahead while handing us the tools for realizing our own fuller potentials.

This book, written about her experiences, is important not only because it entertains and instructs us, but because it validates experiences that in spite of recent progress are not widely validated by our society. The author gives courage and support to readers whose intuitive capacities are awakening. Hopefully, you will be one of them.

Today our world is rapidly moving beyond our two-hundred-year romance with Newtonian physics that sees the universe and the human mind as machines. As British astronomer James Jeans said nearly seventy years ago, the universe of the modem physicist looks much more like a great thought than a giant supermachine. Along with tearing away old veils to the world's wisdom, we are looking with new respect at people who have already developed mental and spiritual tools to guide us into the emerging age.

Long ago someone said that we learn best by watching those who are ahead of us. Linda has been wonderfully generous in sharing with us her life during her early emergence. The generosity of that act can carry us all into making this transition in our own lives and doing it with renewed confidence that will allow us, like Linda, to share our own creative and intuitive gifts with the world.

Hal Zina Bennett, Ph.D.
1998

Hal Zina Bennett is the author of more than twenty-eight successful books on intuition, creativity, spiritual development, and healing.

Preface

Headlines and surveys have told us that many Americans admit they believe in angels. More and more people speak of their lives being assisted by angels, spirit guides, or other invisible helpers. We hear people say, "If I hadn't heard that little voice whispering in my ear, I wouldn't be alive today," or some similar statement. Undoubtedly, there is at least one person in your neighborhood who communicates with nonphysical friends but doesn't want to talk about it for fear of being laughed at or considered crazy.

When I risked that ridicule by discussing my communication with spiritual beings on national radio and television, it became obvious to me how important it is for everyone who has psychic experiences to bring them out into the open. I received a great deal of feedback from people who, by learning about my experiences, decided they weren't crazy after all. By making myself vulnerable on various talk shows, I also discovered that many people can get aggressive about the subject of having a private relationship with an intangible being. It became obvious to me how it is more important than ever for all human beings to be able to redefine the psychic experience and bring it closer to the heart so it isn't so frightening.

Secretly, lots of "normal, down-to-earth folks" are not only developing valuable friendships with spirit beings, but are also exploring new territories of the human psyche, seeking to understand the vast mysteries of the immaterial world. Intuition Magic is designed as a road map to assist the inward-venturing seeker within this immaterial world of intuition and spirituality.

I have called this book *Intuition Magic* because through the development of our intuitive perception, we can unlock the magical inner power that enables us to sense, enjoy, and learn from the immaterial but infinitely fantastic part of our universe.

We need not always be shackled to the work desk by our logical, reasoning minds. By developing and trusting our intuition, we can be free to explore the parts of our world that nurture our spirit in ways that transcend rational explanations.

That people on a massive scale have a willing tendency to admit to believing in angels and other invisible friends suggests that humans are finally beginning to trust in their intuitive knowledge. This is an important step toward creating harmony and balance in our lives, as we begin to treat Planet Earth as one living, breathing, nurturing organism that can sustain and enrich us all-if only we could feel safe enough to trust in the truth of our intuitive spiritual nature and drop our deep skepticism and fears.

It is my intention with *Intuition Magic* to help you unveil the spiritual aspects of your world in a simple and playful manner. It was after much frustration in my own spiritual quest that I decided a book with this approach was desperately needed.

This revelation came to me many years ago while in a metaphysical bookstore in Amsterdam. Among the Eastern spiritual texts, both modern and ancient, I came upon a book with a chart in it showing the various planes of human consciousness. As I read about the Buddhic plane, I began to feel hopelessly boring and ordinary. I stood thinking to myself: "It doesn't help to tell people about all of those planes of consciousness. It just makes them feel stupid."

After that experience, I struggled to get some of my self-confidence back. Then, I realized that the individuals who had written many of those texts had never actually discovered the spiritual insights or phenomena they were writing about. They were simply translating what had been passed on through the ages. The roots of their material were undoubtedly very real and pure, but as soon as this information had been written down, intellectualized, and translated into Western concepts, it had lost most of its power to teach.

First hand experience was gone. I imagined that it must be an infinitesimal few who knew how to integrate nirvana into their daily lives.

There are countless miracles outside and inside us that we are rigidly conditioned to ignore from the moment we are born, so that our intuitive self is often pushed away to a seemingly impassable distance. We struggle to feel it from a second- or third-hand perspective, but, in reality, this greater dimension of our lives is closer and more accessible than most people dare to believe.

I have designed *Intuition Magic* not only to acquaint you with some new ideas, but also to give you a complete hands-on experience, providing concepts and exercises you can put to use right away. This book is divided into two parts. The first half is a narrative in which I explain how I accumulated knowledge about intuition and spirituality. Part II of the book is an experiential workshop that will let you explore the world intuitively, discover your own spiritual helpers, and understand new dimensions about yourself and others.

For clarity, and to compress my experiences into a handy volume, I have created characters in my narrative that are composites, representing several students and teachers with whom I have been associated—both at the schools where I first took my training and at Mens & Intuitie (People & Intuition) in the Netherlands, which I founded.

It is my hope that by reading *Intuition Magic,* you will understand what intuitive development means on a practical, daily-life basis and realize it is not beyond your capabilities. I offer you this information in the belief that you can, without a doubt, learn to trust in the intangible world and all the miracles and magic to be witnessed on this plane of human reality. May you receive and savor these experiences, thereby deeply enriching your everyday life.

Acknowledgments

Heartfelt gratitude to David Ciaffardini,
Brandt Morgan, Gaelyn Larrick, and Hal Zina
Bennett, for their skilled assistance and loving
support in the final stages.

PART ONE

THE AWAKENING

Chapter One

Cosmic Brick Wall

As a child, I remember sitting in church—not listening to the minister, but staring out the stained-glass windows. There, I found myself in another world where I was appreciated beyond words. As I grew older, I discovered that not everybody experienced the Sunday service the way I did. Even up to the time I went to college, I still hoped to find other people to whom I could relate my spiritual eccentricities. I chose anthropology and archaeology as majors because I thought I would find like-minded people who were as fascinated as I was with the rituals and ceremonies of ancient cultures. It was obvious to me that these original peoples had tapped into a source of earthly and cosmic magic that totally supported their world and gave their lives great meaning. My studies, however mentally and socially invigorating, did not help to enrich my understanding of spirituality or the original magic of human beings. I realized that I needed to venture out on my own if I expected to find any more information on this subject.

For this reason I joined a small, close-knit group of seekers who got together regularly to discuss and explore various aspects of spirituality. We meditated, chanted, and spoke of our dreams with each other. The year I spent with these earnest seekers was a year of continuous revelation for me. I became aware that life had a great secret inner structure that I had never fully comprehended. I also discovered vast territories of my psyche I had never known existed.

Despite my spiritual work with this group, I came up against what I call a two-layer cosmic brick wall. The first layer was a lonely dichotomy, with everyday life seeming so separate from my private spiritual world. In my meditations, I could travel to heavenly, jeweled palaces seeking enlightenment, while the next moment I would find myself in a battered yellow Volkswagen, caught in rush hour traffic, breathing exhaust fumes, and late for work. The deeper I became involved in the psychic-spiritual dimension, the more alienated I felt from the rest of reality. I found it difficult to explain my initiations and other spiritual activities and interests to most of my friends. I kept my metaphysical self incognito, feeling odd and left out, afraid I would be judged as someone who had been brainwashed or turned into a religious fanatic.

The second layer of the cosmic brick wall was my inability to turn my sensitivity off when I wanted to. Through continual effort, I was willfully opening my doors to inner perception. I didn't realize that these entrances were letting in many unwanted messages from the outside, causing me great confusion, fear, and unhappiness. It was as if my mind were constantly being cluttered with psychic junk mail.

My breakthrough began when I went to a party and met Jeannie, a fascinating woman I was drawn to immediately. After we met, there was really no party left for me, but simply the two of us communicating. I don't recall how we started on the subject, but soon we were talking about human auras, the energy fields that surround our bodies. I believed I had an aura, but I had hardly thought about it, nor did I know what it did.

To help me understand, my new friend told me to close my eyes and tell what colors I saw around her right hand. I shut my eyes and, without hesitation, told her I saw green and yellow. Then she asked me what colors I saw around her left hand. I told her green and yellow with a little bit of blue.

"Now close your eyes and tell me what colors you see around your own hands," she said.

I told her what I saw and began feeling quite pleased with myself.

"This is great! But what's the point?" I asked.

"You've been looking at both of our auras."

"What? No," I protested. "It can't be. I was just imagining those colors."

"Well, your imagination is something, you know. It's not just a useless inner appendage."

We both laughed. As silly and nervous as I felt, I was ready to believe her. I knew the visualizations I practiced during my many meditations were real and could manifest themselves on a physical level. When I visualized vital energies rising up my spine, I could feel my spine tingling; when I concentrated upon my so-called third eye between my eyebrows, I would feel a warm glow at my forehead. Yet until that evening, seeing an aura was something I had considered beyond my abilities, something that only psychics or gurus were capable of. From Jeannie, I realized the reason I had never seen an aura was because I had never *looked* for one!

While we talked, a friend walked over and explained that Jeannie was clairvoyant and a student at a school for intuitive development.

"You can call it clairvoyance," Jeannie smiled, "but you can also call it clear seeing. You were being clairvoyant a few minutes ago when you looked at our hands and saw colors."

Jeannie continued offering bits of metaphysical information about me that were astounding. She told me I was a very ungrounded person and thereby found it difficult to accomplish things in spite of my best intentions. She told me I needed to learn how to ground myself so that I wouldn't be soaring in confusion after my meditations. Her advice was comforting. Why hadn't I ever thought of it this way?

Jeannie reminded me about chakras, energy centers in the body that I had become familiar with during previous spiritual studies.

"I'm noticing something that could cause you a great deal of confusion," she explained. "Your second chakra is wide open, making you much too vulnerable emotionally. You easily experience the emotions of other people and then think they're your own. This is what's keeping you from knowing your true self and your soul's purpose."

What Jeannie was telling me seemed accurate. But her message began to make me feel inadequate, realizing that my meditations, which I valued so much, had left me metaphysically crippled. It irritated me to realize that a virtual stranger understood my psychic system better than I did. I implored her to tell me more, and she mentioned a group of people who got together several times a week.

"It's a kind of meditation class where we're trying to find out more about our intuitive abilities," she explained. She wrote a phone number on a scrap of paper, handed it to me with a big smile, and told me it was time for her to go home. At the time, I didn't realize how much that phone number would change my life.

Chapter Two

Exploding Roses

Several months passed before I got the nerve to call the school where Jeannie studied intuitive development. An assistant told me their classes had grown so large that they were being taught in several different locations. The school had doubled in size since I had met Jeannie! I was given details about the cost and location of the beginning classes and picked a time to enroll.

One afternoon several weeks later; I left my household of Irish musicians to attend my first class, rocketing myself from one universe to another. On entering the classroom, I saw a group of about twenty people who looked as nervous and perplexed as I felt. Yet, with the sun streaming in through the windows and the friendly people greeting us, our anxiety quickly melted away. We each took a seat in a large circle of chairs.

The next thing I knew, there was a woman standing in front of me doing funny things with her hands. She said she was giving me a healing. Our teacher, a man in his thirties named Tom, had five assistants who were performing that same strange ritual before each person in the room. I had no idea what was going on. I didn't think I needed to be healed of anything, but I kept quiet. To my surprise, I could feel something flowing out of the healer's hands even though she wasn't touching me. Then, when she laid her hands on my feet, I could feel a current of warmth. She continued by putting her hands above my upturned palms, and I felt a prickling in my arms and hands. When she finally moved to the next person, I felt like a little kid who had just been cared for by a kindly, old-fashioned doctor. But I still wondered if all the sensations I felt were just a product of my imagination.

Tom explained at that moment, as if he had heard what I had been thinking, how our imagination can be a means of perceiving a reality that is invisible, yet as real as our physical bodies. "When we start valuing our imagination, it enables us to see the whole of life, not just a collection of random particles," Tom said. "It can enable us to see life for what it really is—one living organism of which we all are a substantial part."

"How about using my imagination simply to have fun and be creative?" an older woman asked.

"Right," Tom said. "In order to reach your creative potential, you definitely need access to your imagination. This neglected skill is the main vehicle for manifesting needs and desires. Unfortunately, most of us leave our creative imagination rusting in the garage of our intellect."

Tom gave us some exercises that involved visualizing specific images. Because of my previous training, visualization came easily to me. I recalled the times I had meditated, imagining I could fly out the window, soaring into obscure, celestial realms, feeling free and elated. However, coming back into my body had often been a shock, both mentally and physically. Not only would my recurring backache still be with me, it would feel worse. I wondered what I might have been doing wrong.

"Remember, meditating doesn't mean you have to leave your body," Tom explained gently. "Instead, you invite divine consciousness into your body."

I feared that my training in Eastern meditation techniques was going to be more of a hindrance than a help. It dawned on me how spaced-out all my previous meditations had been.

"Imagine a rose right in front of you," Tom instructed. "Take a look at its roots and make sure it's grounded in
the earth. Take a close look at the rose. Is it just budding or
opened all the way? Does it have lots of leaves or just a few?
What about the thorns? Now have this rose disappear in
front of you, without effort, in a tiny explosion."

To an outsider, it would have looked like a very
boring class, what with everybody's eyes closed as if we
were taking naps. Yet from the inside, we were as involved
as any delighted crew of explorers discovering new and
foreign shores.

"Allow yourself the freedom and luxury of creating
something with your imagination, then without effort, let it
go," Tom told us. "You're not being destructive when you let
go of something you created with your imagination. Being
able to receive and then let go of an image is an art—something that establishes your freedom as a creative being."

After we were led out of our meditative state, an unhealthy looking middle-aged man told us he wondered how
he could have lived his life without experiencing this inner
freedom. Nearly everyone agreed, and all eyes remained
fixed on our instructor.

Tom continued to talk about the value of visualization. He said that forming any sort of image with our eyes
closed could be difficult, since most people lose this important ability somewhere around the first grade.

"After kindergarten, thinking was in and imagination was out!" Tom proclaimed. "How many of you got into
trouble for daydreaming at school? It was probably around
the first grade that many of you began losing your creative
inner world to all the standard, acceptable forms of learning
imposed from the outside. Now we're going to go back to
that first grade and connect with all those threads of fantasy
and imagination that can keep you directly in touch with
the deeper, intuitive you—a source of truth that can tell you

so much, about your relationship with the rest of the world.

"During meditation, I want you to use your imagination in a creative way," Tom went on. "You don't necessarily have to see anything. You can experience feelings, sensations, ideas, and moods without any mental pictures: Having so-called visions is much less common than the simple phenomenon I've just described. Don't be disappointed if the experience of visualization is not as dramatic as you had expected."

Everything Tom was describing sounded so routine—almost disappointingly so.

"But," I uttered, "I always thought I'd need a vision, something very real and convincing, in order to have a genuinely psychic experience."

"Don't get hung up on the spectacular aspects of psychic experiences," he replied. "Most of what you're going to learn here will seem pretty ordinary, especially once you've mastered it. However, your ability to create pictures with your imagination sets the stage for creating your own reality. Being able to visualize is not only being able to *receive* mental-image pictures, it's also being able to *create* and *project* them. Your world of imagination is not simply childish fantasy; it's your most powerful tool to perceive, observe, and eventually transform energy patterns."

Tom glanced at his watch and told us we were running out of time, then quickly reminded us that the "rose mock-up" was the most important exercise to practice. Our homework for the week was to sit down for a few minutes each day and create, inside ourselves, all the colors, shapes, and sizes of roses we could imagine. Then, as soon as each rose was complete in our mind, we were supposed to let it go.

Chapter Three

Feeling Auras

The second meditation class started very much like the first. Each of us received healings, which mainly had to do with cleaning our auras. We learned that we all have a personal field of energy around us that, like any home, needs routine cleaning. The assistants doing the healings were students, and I was impressed with how easily they told me bits of truth about myself:

"You certainly are ungrounded. I'm going to connect you up much better to the earth. . . . You have all sorts of expectations from others in your energy field. . . . It looks as if you find it difficult to make good separations between yourself and others. . . . There's a lot of creative energy coming from your hands. Do you play a musical instrument?"

I accepted it all with a curious smile. These assistants made cleaning auras seem as routine as picking up after yourself.

Tom told us the healers were using various levels of intuition to "feel out" this information, and that it was an extremely simple process. I wasn't convinced. I was sure they must be psychic adepts. I felt self-conscious, afraid they would see more about me than I was ready to reveal.

Later, as an exercise in developing our intuitive abilities, we students were asked to practice feeling each other's auras. We paired off and stood a few feet away from each other. As I moved uneasily toward my partner, I was astounded to feel something odd—like a charge or subtle force—surrounding her. It was something I wouldn't have noticed unless I had been told to try it. With shock, I realized I just had touched my partner's aura!

"Remember to keep your attention inside yourself so you don't get mixed up with each other's energy," Tom explained. "Feel yourself being receptive and neutral. Your hands may feel warmth or tingling. Be open to any way you happen to experience it."

While feeling my partner's aura, I got a strong sense of how large it was by walking toward the person from a distance and then feeling the outside boundaries. I discovered the aura had different layers that extended in different ways, not only in size but also in force. Following the contours to the ground, I noticed much less energy around the legs and feet. Many others were noticing this same phenomenon, and the room was buzzing with excitement.

I totally forgot Tom's instructions to stay focused inside myself. I was becoming lost in this captivating world while probing the aura layers closest to my partner's body. Suddenly my partner got irritated and broke my attention. The nearest assistant noticed this and acknowledged us with a subdued grin.

"What happened just now," she said to me, "is that you were feeling the layers of the aura closest to the body for too long without being centered. That can become annoying to your partner."

My partner and I laughed and decided it was time to switch. Now it was my turn to have my aura touched. In this role, I could listen better to the teacher's explanations about the auric field.

"Realize that the human aura is constantly changing, even at this moment when you're working with your partner," Tom said. "It varies with mood, health conditions, and surroundings. Remember that your aura is your very own psychic territory to know, to keep clear, to protect, and to make totally yours. Where your aura ends and the rest of the world begins is your psychic boundary."

I looked at the other students and noticed that some of them were perplexed, while others were going about their business of aura-feeling as if they had been waiting for permission to do it all their lives.

"Not only does your aura tell lots of things about you," Tom explained, "but it constantly takes on mental pictures and information from the outside world. If you want to know yourself better, you need to be able to tell what information is coming from you and what information is coming from people you're in contact with. That's why it's important to regularly clean out your aura—your own psychic space—in order to see more clearly what's going on."

For homework, we were to continue to create and explode roses in front of us and continue to get in touch with our own aura and those of others.

I left class thinking that, like all my previous spiritual training, this was an adventure into an unknown world of subtle messages and delicate observations. But unlike my previous experiences, I was beginning to understand the practicality of intuitive information. The most difficult aspect was to trust my own information. Yet Tom kept telling us we were simply coming into contact with the framework of a different reality. Once we became more familiar with this level of reality, we could integrate it more comfortably with levels that were more familiar to us. In this way, we could begin to make desired changes in ourselves and have more control over the course of our lives.

Chapter Four

Hello, Earth

During the following week, I noticed how difficult it was to integrate these new psychic experiences into my daily routines. I was often irritable and felt out of touch with others in my household. Sometimes I would burst into laughter or tears and not know why.

When I went to my next class, I was relieved to hear that the problems I was experiencing were normal. Tom explained that, as part of the solution, we were going to learn to ground ourselves. For a variety of reasons, he said, many people are poorly connected to the earth. One common reason, especially for people involved in psychic and spiritual development, is that they frequently leave their bodies looking for answers. The problem is that many people continue to stay "out" and lose concern for their physical bodies. This can create an inability to accomplish anything or finish a task. It can also cause ill health.

"Enough brain food for now," Tom said, standing up. "It's time to experience the earth. Imagine her as a colored globe and say hello. What color or colors do you see and how do they feel?" This was a cinch for me. I could finally float above our earthly reality as I used to in meditation.

"If your picture of our planet is a pleasant one, keep it like that," Tom said. "If your picture is less pleasant, you can, with your imagination, give it more color. Picture the earth in such a way that you can feel a fine connection with it. Affirm to yourself that it's really a wonderful place to be."

I imagined paradise on earth and became emotional. "Now come back into your body and direct your attention to the base of your spine," Tom went on. "Imagine that from out of your spine extends a golden beam of energy going down through your chair through the floor. As it touches the earth, this golden beam of energy is going to say 'Hello, Earth!' It will continue to move deeper into the earth, through all of her layers, until it finally comes to the very center."

There was silence as everyone imaginatively delved into the depths of the planet.

"Allow your golden energy beam to make a connection with the center of the earth in any way that feels good to you," Tom said. "You now have a powerful energy line going from the base of your spine to the center of the earth. We call this your grounding cord. Your grounding cord can be made of anything you like. It can be golden roots growing out of your spine. It can be a laser beam, a rope, a tube, a wooden pole, a tail—whatever feels good to you."

"It makes me feel all nervous and panicky," one very thin woman piped up. "W hat am I supposed to do now!"

"That's because you're not used to it yet," Tom calmly assured. "Sometimes new things that are good for us make us feel very uncomfortable in the beginning, just because they're so new. Give yourself plenty of time and space to adjust to the changes."

After class, while talking to a fellow student, I noticed that my comfortable grounding cord seemed to have disappeared entirely. I felt lost and drifting, like a ship without an anchor. The class assistant was still around, so I decided to ask about it.

"It's great that you noticed the difference so soon," she said. "It takes time to learn how to maintain your grounding while doing other things. It's one thing to be with yourself in meditation and quite another to be out in the world. Don't worry, it'll evolve more rapidly than you might expect."

The next week we were given more exercises to increase our groundedness. We were told to visualize a stream of earth energy flowing up through our feet and legs to our first chakra at the base of our spine.

"Grounding is more than a platitude or an idealistic visualization," Tom explained. "It's a very potent tool, a way in which you and Planet Earth can communicate with each other. You may see the earth simply as a big, solid ball rotating around the sun, sustaining life on its surface. Or you can see the earth as a living, breathing organism—a conscious entity with which you can communicate. Allow yourself to sense the latter for a moment. Say hello to Mother Earth when you ground yourself. The earth has its own wisdom and consciousness that you can communicate with."

Tom had put on some beautiful quiet music. I had never felt the earth in this way. I was deeply moved by this homecoming.

"Now ask the center of the earth to say hello to your soul. Imagine the spirit of the earth to be like a giant mother you can always trust, a mother who will comfort and nourish you."

I was impressed by the idea that the physical body— and the physical world in general—were objects deserving great reverence. How different this was from other religious philosophies I had come across, many of which express disdain for our physical reality.

"Symbolically speaking, your body is the stem of your own lotus flower, which represents your spiritual awakening," Tom explained. "When you ground, it reminds you that you live on a planet that has a force called gravity. If you let go of something, it will fall naturally toward the center of the earth. To ground yourself, then, is one of the most natural things you can do."

When I grounded myself, I felt a stream of earth

energy flowing from the earth into my legs. It was as if my feet had little suction cups on the bottom that were pumping the energy upward. However, others in the class were not as fortunate. One man sat in his chair looking totally frustrated.

"I don't feel a damned thing!" he said loudly.

"Don't worry about it," answered Tom. "Something will surely come of it. Just give it a chance."

The grumbling man looked a little more hopeful, and Tom's statement became something I would repeat to myself for a long time to come: "Just give it a chance. Just give it a chance."

Chapter Five

Becoming Free

After the fourth class, I felt it was imperative that I absorb every piece of information being taught at the school. I was also extremely curious about the origins of these teachings and was thrilled when I was finally able to meet Kitty, one of the mysterious founders of the school.

Kitty was a pretty, middle-aged woman with sparkling, blue-green eyes and long brown hair highlighted with streaks of gray. When she entered the room, I felt conspicuous towering above her small, delicate body.

"I guess you're one of those new students, huh? They seem to get bigger every day!" she quipped, a twinkle in her eye. I had the impression Kitty had a tremendous amount of wisdom to share, but wouldn't dump the whole heap on my head at one sitting. I would soon learn how extremely patient she was and what a knack she had for knowing how much information a person could use at any given time.

Despite her position of authority and seeming omniscience, she was never condescending and was relentless only with her humor and jovial spirit. However, one day during the first months of my study, while I was sitting next to her on the couch after class, she turned to me, looking very serious.

"You know, Linda, you're not here to become psychic or clairvoyant or anything like that," she said. "You're here to become free."

I was impressed with her statement, and after that felt more at peace attending her school. I was learning to trust my intuition to improve the quality of my life, not to become somebody special or fall into any ego game.

Kitty had been a professional actress and had taught at a number of acting schools. As a girl, she had had very strong intuitive abilities. Later in her life, she had informally instructed friends and acquaintances in the use of clairvoyance, healing, and intuitive perception in general. After retiring from her acting career, she had devoted herself full-time (along with her partner, Bill) to establishing a school for intuitive development.

Bill was not much taller than Kitty. His dark, curly hair encircled his bald head like a wreath. His cheeks were rosy from pure enthusiasm, and he was always ready for the next laugh. Kitty and Bill told us that people they helped casually and for free often became too dependent on them. These experiences had persuaded them to set up a formal, tuition-based school that would encourage people to become responsible for their own learning.

The system of learning at the school was strikingly different from any I had ever encountered. There wasn't a book anywhere, and learning was done entirely through firsthand experience. As soon as a student learned some of the basics, he or she would share this with new students. This system had a twofold function. The more-advanced students would become more proficient with acquired skills, and the newer students would receive personalized help and attention.

Besides offering classes, the school provided aura readings given by graduates and near graduates. Those who came for readings usually wanted to get in touch with their intuitive potentials or discover how their psychic attitudes related to the physical world. The information these seekers were given always had to do with the same concept: know yourself better and gain control over your life.

At Kitty and Bill's insistence, each beginning student had to help perform these public readings at least twice a week, practicing the techniques they had learned in classes and lectures. Taking part in the readings was the most painful experience I encountered at the school. Because of my lack of confidence, many times I left the place in tears, utterly frustrated. But eventually, as my teachers predicted, these painful problems proved to be blessings in disguise.

As students, we would spend half our time attending lectures and classes and the other half learning to give psychic readings. The most intense learning seemed to occur during the readings, yet the groundwork was established in the meditation classes. Some classes were combined with more advanced students; others were comprised simply of our group of twelve beginners. Whether in class or during a reading, we spent most of our time observing the ways we had been taught to think about life and ourselves— and looking at the things that prevented us from learning and growing.

Kitty and Bill's favorite way of starting a discussion was to ask us to search for the illusions that kept us imprisoned—for instance, blaming others for our own problems. Kitty and Bill explained that this attitude diverted us from taking responsibility for our situations. We were shown what a mistake it is to blame other people for our failures and misfortunes.

Another important concept they introduced was that the mental images we carry inside us define and dictate what we can and cannot do.

"If you can go one step above the picture and look more objectively, you can literally discard the pictures that are bothering you," Kitty explained. "Just like you made those roses disappear during the first class. It can be that simple."

Kitty told us that to become free, we needed to learn to "explode" pictures. We needed to learn how to neutralize any mental images that controlled us and created realities that made us feel unhappy.

"During the early years of our lives, we collect a certain amount of emotionally charged pictures that govern the way we use our energy," she said. "This is how we create a belief system. For instance, if you were raised to believe you don't deserve what you want in this life, those emotionally charged images would blind you from seeing any information that contradicts that negative belief. Even if everyone around you showed respect and appreciated you, you wouldn't feel it because you wouldn't believe it was true. You create your experiences, either positive or negative, with the mental images you hold on to. When you change your pictures and beliefs, you ultimately change yourself and the reality around you. My intention is to teach you how to work toward your own personal freedom."

"Say hello to your problems!" Bill exclaimed during class one day. "Your problems are your best friends."

"You've got to be kidding," I blurted, still too ignorant to understand. "Why on earth should I love my problems?"

"Because they're your teachers, that's why!" Bill said. "They give you a chance to learn something new. But make sure you aren't just trying to escape the problem instead of solving it. Notice how much resistance you have regarding your problems. Try accepting situations and ask yourself, 'What am I trying to tell myself?' When you see a problem, say hello to it. Loving your problems allows you to get through them much faster: You'll be very pleasantly surprised."

Chapter Six

Pinkish-Orange

The movie of my life outside the school was turning into a comedy: everything had gone topsy-turvy. I had been trying to maintain the status quo, continuing my life as an office worker, moonlighting as a fiddle teacher, and performing regularly with our band in the local Irish pubs. I loved my musician friends and felt I needed their unspoken assurance that the basics of life could remain uncomplicated.

Yet, when I began to look at my daily existence with new vision, not much was making sense anymore. I was critical of myself and those around me. I was starting to wonder what was real—this comfortable life I had made for myself, or the futuristic, fairytale life I was living at Bill and Kitty's school.

To make matters worse, I was having an impulsive relationship with a wonderful Irishman who tended to drink a lot. He had a magical charm that penetrated the hearts of everyone around him and was as naturally intuitive as everyone at my school put together. His tragedy was that he had been brought up to fear and despise his psychic abilities. His intuition, instead of being a welcome gift, had become something to fear.

This man represented the biggest irony in my life. How could anyone so talented, so funny, and so loving be so miserable? Try to tell him or the rest of my household friends about auras, exploding pictures, and belief systems,

33

and see how far that would get me!

It seemed about time to get a psychic reading from a graduate of the school. I hadn't dared to arrange for a reading before because I had been concerned about its emotional impact. I was nervous and afraid of what might be revealed. What secrets might stream, unchecked, from my subconscious?

When I finally entered the reading room, I saw the familiar three people sitting in chairs. These were the readers—a graduate reader in the center chair and two undergraduates on either side of him. Next to them was a small table with a tape recorder on it. An empty chair was facing them. All three aura readers had their eyes closed, silently preparing to observe my aura and chakras. Another student was going to be the watchdog, or "control," making sure the atmosphere in the room remained as comfortable and light as possible.

As I sat down in the unoccupied chair, I noticed a definite quality of tension and nervousness. I wondered how much of it was coming from me. The three newer students would probably be feeling unsure of themselves, as usual. The control walked around the room, occasionally approaching one of the readers to suggest that he or she ground better or remember to breathe deeply. The atmosphere in the room slowly became more comfortable.

The reader in the center chair rubbed her hands together as if trying to warm them up. With her eyes closed, she held her left palm facing me, moving her fingers ever so slightly. I knew she was using the chakra in the palm of her hand to receive information. After silently scanning me with her hand for several minutes, she began to speak.

"Would you please say your full name several times?"

I repeated my name, knowing that by listening to the way I spoke, she could see pictures or colors, or otherwise sense information about me.

"What I'm going to talk about first, Linda," the reader said with her eyes still closed, "is a set of symbols I've visualized in front of me. I'm allowing your energy to flow into them. This gives me a great deal of information about you, both as a personality and as an immortal being. It helps me to communicate with you very directly.

"A rose is the central figure in this picture," she went on, "and it symbolizes you for right now. I'm seeing your rose at this time to be a pinkish orange. To me, this color represents a kind of outgoingness and creative attitude. There's an intense golden area in the center of the rose, which means to me that you are sometimes able to focus your concentration and creative abilities to a very high degree. However, right above this rose on the left side, I see a darkish-blue cloud with a bit of red around it. It looks like that blue is your fear of what other people will think of you if you express your creative power too openly. You're too much afraid of what other people think of you. That red on the edge of the cloud looks like the pain involved in this process. You're getting hurt because you're often fighting against your own true nature. You're losing lots of focus because of this."

The reader shifted slightly in her chair. "Now I'm looking at your rose in relation to the sun in this picture, to determine how much you are in touch with your higher self. I see it's turned about halfway toward the sun. Your rose is very open, yet it's not always leaning toward direct communication with your higher self. Do you have any questions so far?"

"It makes a lot of sense," I answered. "But how deeply established is this pattern? I feel somewhat restricted by this picture. I wonder how long it will take me to change it."

"To tell you the truth," the reader said, smiling at me with closed eyes, "you could come back here in a few months or so and show me an entirely different rose. But everybody's got to have some opposing aspects to their rose. That's how we learn. So don't try to be perfect. You'd do a lot better if you'd just let yourself be exactly who you are. The story depicted by your rose is what you've got to work with now. It's your way of learning. Besides, you should be terribly pleased with all of that pinkish-orange and golden energy. It's helping you tremendously."

I realized she was right and told myself to be more appreciative of my pinkish-orange and gold.

"Your aura is strong and healthy, but it's not going down all the way to the ground," the reader continued. "You're really not owning your poor feet very much. This could make it difficult for you to ground properly. Would you like me to try to bring your aura down more around your legs and feet?"

"Sure," I said cheerfully. "You have my permission."

I knew the reader was going to imagine my aura moving downward, and that the power of her thoughts would actually have an effect on my energy field. I knew she had invisible healing helpers and personal guardians who were directly in contact with her during the entire reading. Somehow I could sense their presence, as well as the presence of the helping guides belonging to everyone else in the room. The room was literally brimming with spiritual guardians hovering in readiness to help and heal.

I watched as the reader waved her hands slowly, sending healing energies to the appropriate places.

"It looks like you're storing fear and negative energy in your feet," she said finally.

This sounded silly to me. "Why in the world would I put it there?" I replied.

"You've got to dump it somewhere. You haven't yet learned how to neutralize your negative thoughts and fears to stop this habit."

"Is this why I've got cold feet most of the time?"

"Sure looks like it. You're not allowing enough of your own energy into them yet. Try more grounding exercises. The next class will help you out, since you'll be learning to bring in your sun essence. But for now, make those feet yours and love them! Respect the wisdom of your feet and legs. Sometimes they know where to take you when your rational mind becomes too cluttered and confused to know."

With the help of her guardians, the reader spent more time cleaning my aura, getting rid of all the extraneous energy hanging around me: She was doing a psychic housecleaning for my general well-being.

"I see much more brightness in your aura now," she said when she was finished. "You're much more yourself now, and living more in present time as well. Do you notice the difference?"

Indeed, I was feeling exceptionally clear and calm. At this point, the undergraduate readers added bits of information that complemented what she had already told me.

Now it was time for a break, and we all went downstairs for a cup of tea. I was feeling very happy. It amused me to think that all these people were spending their time and attention just for me. I felt like I was being initiated into a native tribe by a throng of wise, old medicine people.

Chapter Seven

Step by Step

The second half of the reading was set aside for viewing and healing my chakras and answering my questions. The reader immediately noticed that my first chakra was not well grounded. She told me my lifestyle appeared to be chaotic because of it. She also said that many of the colors she saw in my first chakra were dark and heavy.

"People with an ungrounded first chakra are often frustrated as they attempt to manifest creativity on a physical level," she said. "This often shows up in their efforts to earn money. It appears you're struggling with financial security, like it's something you don't feel safe or sure about yet."

I nodded in agreement.

"I'm trying to neutralize some of that dense energy by bringing earth energy into your legs," she explained."At the same time, I'm going to send some of your own nice pinkish-orange color there. Also some green to help the healing process."

I could feel a tingling at the base of my spine and began to laugh nervously. Next came the second chakra, which I intuitively felt was one of my biggest trouble spots. After a few minutes of inspection in my belly area, the reader asked me if I had been practicing celibacy.

I had to grin. "Well, yes, actually, I said. "I belonged to a spiritual group, and it was the thing to do. But that was three years ago."

"Well, you might be surprised to know that I can see a shield of protection around your second chakra," she said. "It looks like a strong invalidation of your sexual energy. It's not so strong anymore, but that phase of your life certainly made a big impression on you."

I sat pondering for a moment. "I thought I had gotten rid of most of those pictures," I said. "But I'll admit that I'm still not sure of my intentions when it comes to intimate relationships."

"You know," the reader said gently, "if you don't accept yourself on all levels, including your sexuality, you're going to be denying significant aspects of the total you. You've got some wonderful, clear colors in your second chakra area that tell me your emotional life comes easily and naturally. You might consider using that natural ability in a happy and positive way rather than denying it."

"I didn't think I was denying it," I replied, slightly upset. "I thought I was channeling that energy up into my heart and upper chakras."

The reader shook her head and smiled kindly. "Why should you do it that way? Your heart and upper chakras can have as much energy as they need simply by being what they are. Each chakra has its own purpose and potential. No one chakra is more important than another."

"That's what I'm finally learning," I sighed. "But I also know I have a real problem with relationships. I can feel so much emotion that I think I'm in love, but then it often turns out to be unrealistic. I honestly don't know what to do with my feelings."

"In order to get more objective about it, you could first become more aware of how you're using your emotions and sexual energy," the reader said. "You know from your classes that you can close that second chakra down somewhat rather than disown it or deny what it's telling you. You're confused there, because you think it's bad to have certain feelings. But you have no choice about it. The feelings are there. The important thing is what you do with them. You need to own and respect all of your feelings, whether you consider them positive or negative. Behind each feeling is an important message about yourself.

"To make things more complicated, Linda, you're so ungrounded at times that once you allow your emotions to come through, you can quickly become carried away by them. You seem to be going from one relationship to the next without success. You need to become more objective about your emotional life. Just remember, you created your life this way in order to learn. It doesn't matter how long it takes you to change your stuck patterns. What's important is to take it step by step, to be patient in the process, and to work every day on your grounding, OK?"

By this time I felt completely depressed, but I tried to pretend I wasn't. The next topic of discussion was the third chakra. I knew it was located at my solar plexus and represented the physical distribution of the life-force energy.

"You're very open here, and you're leaking a lot of energy," the reader said. "You need to collect your energies more often. I see you leaving your energy scattered about the countryside!"

I immediately thought of when I played music in the pubs, and how horribly tired and exhausted I would feel afterward. The reader gave me a special exercise to retrieve my lost life force. I was to imagine having a kind of magnet in my stomach area. I thought this would be very useful. Then she went on to the fourth chakra.

"Your fourth chakra, the heart chakra, is very open, yet it seems to be in a state of confusion," she said. "You're keeping many lines of communication open to many people at once. You feel you can't give any one of them sufficient time or care. You're trying to be too responsible in your concern for others. It's like trying to answer several telephone lines at the same time. It would be helpful to be more in present time and hang up before you make a new call."

"I also see guilt pictures in your heart that have to do

with past unsuccessful relationships. Try to get some clarity on the subject, Linda. And get rid of those guilt pictures! Explode those pictures and start to forgive yourself."

At this point, I couldn't hold in my emotions any longer. The tears began to roll, and we took a familiar "Kleenex break." The "control" in the room came over to comfort me and began to tell a few silly jokes, which caused me to laugh uncontrollably. It was a relief to discuss my problems with people who were so understanding.

Finally, the graduate reader went on to look at my fifth chakra, which is located at the throat. This chakra represents telepathy, the inner voice, and practical intuition. She said I was very open here, too. But, as with my heart chakra, I needed to clean up all the old communication lines and bring myself more into present time.

"You often function on telepathic levels without knowing it," the reader told me. "This causes you to know more than you really want to at times. It can give you problems with those who aren't being honest with you. This can be a terrible source of confusion: you hear one thing but sense another."

She finished off the reading by looking at my sixth chakra, at the forehead, representing clairvoyance and abstract intuition, and at my seventh chakra, at the top of my head, representing intuitive knowledge and autonomy.

"You're open and perceptive in both of these centers, but have difficulty finding your confidence. You still believe other people know more about what's best for you than you do yourself. Be careful not to give up your psychic seniority to others! Your greatest task is to believe more in your own information."

The long reading finally came to an end. Everybody sat silently, cleaning out their auras and making psychic separations from each other. I was glad for tape recorders, since the information and insights seemed to be too much to integrate right away, and I was left swimming in a sea of my own thoughts.

Chapter Eight

Sun Child

I had been told during my reading that our next class would be about the sun essence. Anne, a new teacher, began the class by telling us to imagine a whirlwind spinning gently through our auras—a whirlwind that would collect energy, pictures, ideas, anything that didn't belong to us. We were to let all foreign energies simply fall away into the ground, where they would become easily neutralized.

We were supposed to visualize these things spinning off the top of our heads. After that, Anne taught us to use the symbol of a golden sun shining above us, bringing pure light into our bodies and auras. In this way, we filled ourselves with an energy that symbolized our soul essence, or higher self. She told us we could get in touch with this higher self simply by asking it to be there.

We visualized this image, said hello to it, and tried to feel it as vividly as we could. Getting in touch with our sun was to become one of the most frequently repeated exercises we did in class. Learning how to be on good terms with this vital sun imagery was essential because it represented not only our unique, highest creative soul essence, but also our ability to manifest ourselves in present time.

"Feel your radiant sun shining above your head," Anne said. "See it as a glowing, golden ball of warmth and certainty. This particular sun exists for you and you only. Own your sun and make it totally yours. Have it come into your body, totally filling it with present-time you. Have it fill all the empty spaces in your aura that were taken up by those energies you just cleaned out.

"Now imagine you're in a meadow in springtime, surrounded by trees, with your private sun shining above your head. Suddenly, a beautiful child jumps out of your sun. This carefree child begins running through the meadow, totally free to exist and to fully express itself. The child laughs, dances, sings, jumps up and down, and yells as loudly as possible. Now it runs off and climbs a tree. It's waving to you from high in the branches! Watch as it climbs back down and runs to a small stream and begins to play in the water.

"See the child skipping joyfully back in your direction. It begins to roll around in the soft meadow grass, then lies peacefully in the sunshine. Ask the child to come sit with you—on your lap, or next to you—whatever it wants. Talk to this child."

As I communicated with my child, I felt a wave of joy spreading through my adult body.

"Now let this child become very small," Anne went on. "He or she is going to jump somewhere into your body, wherever it feels the most appropriate. This child lives within you, and you can make contact with it any time you wish."

As we were guided from this vision back to our room, I saw that several people in the group had been crying. This was something we'd become accustomed to, for as we said hello to the hidden layers of ourselves and touched the essence of our creative source, it was often a deeply moving experience. This was true for the men as well as the women. In the beginning, some people had been too embarrassed to cry; however, the longer we knew each other, the easier it became to own up to our emotions in the presence of the group. The more we bared our souls in each other's presence, the more humor abounded and the more fun we had together.

"You see, a child's world is full of playful fantasy," Anne continued. "If a child pretends his bed is a boat, then for him it is really true. Fantasy and reality are an extension of each other, as you've already experienced in your meditations. An imagined grounding cord becomes a real grounding cord that can give you safety and stability both physically and spiritually. You're learning to trust in your ability to visualize, just as a child trusts in its own ability to play.

"Fantasy and trust go side by side, as you can sense when watching a child at play. These childlike abilities have a lot to teach you as you develop your intuition. They allow you to summon vital aspects of your personality that may have been buried for years. Ask those childlike aspects to come out and enrich your life."

"I thought we were learning how to grow up, not act like a child," quipped the university professor in our group.

"We don't have to act like anything. That's the whole point!" Anne retorted. "Most of our true nature is buried under the conditioning we've had all our lives, the conditioning that tells us all the things we should or shouldn't do. Think about it. How much of yourself have you tried to ignore or forget?"

We finished up the class with our own stories of how the exercises had affected us. I told the group how much I had needed this particular lesson to get back in touch with my intuition, and that I was going to do my very best to keep that child alive.

"Don't try too hard!" Anne admonished. "Sometimes too much effort can mislead you from your goals. Effort isn't necessary in *anything* you do! Focus, clarity, and determination are necessary, but don't confuse them with effort; there's an awfully big difference."

"What *is* the difference?" I dared to ask.

Anne looked at me emphatically, "*Trust* is the difference. Everything that happens in our lives is divinely guided if we connect it with the highest good."

Chapter Nine

Fabulous Roses

The symbol embodied in a rose was very important at our school. It was used to protect us, to give us intuitive information quickly and directly, and to make it easier to neutralize mental pictures. I never asked why a rose was used instead of a pansy or a daffodil. But knowing that the rose is considered the queen of all flowers, I figured it had been speaking to people's imaginations for centuries, its innate powers strengthened through the ages by the collective consciousness of humanity.

I had already seen how powerfully the rose symbol worked in an aura reading. Reading a rose symbol was an excellent way of quickly understanding a lot about a person, as I had experienced during my own reading. The roses in various readings appeared in all colors, shapes, and sizes. Some had stems, leaves, and thorns, and these symbols could also be translated into clear messages by the reader. A rose that was just budding could indicate a new cycle of learning and growth. The stem could tell about the person's general attitude toward life. The roots could reveal the ability to manifest deeper desires.

I also learned how the rose symbol could help me stay clear and safe by serving as a psychic buffer. This buffer could be invaluable during readings and in the course of daily life when my psychic boundaries were threatened.

In subsequent classes, we learned how to recognize

when our psychic boundaries were being invaded, and conversely, how to recognize when we were overstepping someone else's boundaries. Our teachers pointed out that if everyone stayed within their own psychic boundaries, there would be little chance of individuals controlling or manipulating each other. If everyone could practice psychic separation and take charge of their own psychic territory, an ideal state of equilibrium would be reached. This equilibrium would enable easy atunement to one's own information and inner voice. In this ideal situation, the teachers explained, confusion disappears.

"Aren't we getting a little too perfect here?" one of my skeptical colleagues asked.

"Don't you see how accustomed we are to invading each others' privacy?" was the teacher's reply. "Humans tell each other what to do because they're afraid of losing control. Can you imagine what it would be like if we began to genuinely respect each other's point of view? Can you imagine what it would be like if each human being were taught to listen with respect to the divine voice within? It would eliminate fear and the need for control.

"Communication is actually enhanced by psychic separation because people are allowed to be themselves," the teacher went on. "When we feel safe and confident, we're much more likely to communicate well."

I practiced this concept at home and tried it out on my alcoholic boyfriend when he blamed me for things I had never done. Normally I would have responded with hostile words and slammed doors as I unknowingly embraced pictures and energies that weren't mine. Instead, envisioning my rose helped produce a neutral state of mind and changed my entire outlook. It allowed me amazing freedom. My calm response heralded a major breakthrough as I suddenly realized that other people's problems weren't necessarily mine. Among other things, I discovered that when my boyfriend was drunk, he liked to say nasty things about me to make himself feel better. Ironically, my newfound neutrality allowed me to respond to him as a helpful friend, without getting caught up in his unfortunate game.

While doing readings for another person, it was extremely helpful to envision several big roses on either side of us, or many little roses around the edges of our auras. It was understood that the roses would absorb any energy, coming from the person getting the reading, that might spill over and cause us to match problems with that person. The protective roses were exceptionally helpful because the power we would ordinarily use to resist other people could be used for our own intuitive perceptions.

The third application of the rose symbol was my favorite. We would neutralize our emotionally charged mental pictures inside a rose and regain our life-force energy and self-awareness.

"It's crucial to see how we are all programmed by our experiences in life," we were reminded by our teachers. "It is definitely possible to reprogram ourselves. One way to reprogram is to neutralize charged pictures, or as we say 'blow pictures.'"

When I had explained this concept to the others in my household, they had smiled at my innocence, thinking I assumed I could change the world with my eyes closed. Back in class, I reported my failure as a missionary, and we all had a good laugh. However, I got some interesting feedback:

"Exploding pictures by neutralizing their emotional charge doesn't always mean they immediately disappear, nor does it mean your problems are miraculously solved," one teacher said. "But it will help you deal with them more constructively because you've become more objective. Using this system of picture awareness reminds you that you are not your pictures."

Although exploding pictures was a simple process, it required the ability to concentrate on a single point. For example, I was actively neutralizing my guilt feelings about my failed relationships. I hadn't gotten rid of all of those guilt feelings, but at least I liked myself more and was becoming more objective about the pictures.

In general, I found that my attitude toward my problems was becoming much lighter. If I kept exploding enough pictures, I believed, I could eventually wipe my slate clean. But like most everyone else, I was also learning the importance of timing and willingness to learn: problems didn't just disappear, but neutralizing pictures certainly helped me to solve them more quickly and easily.

In my private life, I was trying to communicate in different ways, wanting to be as honest as possible with every word that left my mouth. Not that I felt morally obligated; I simply wanted to preserve an enormous amount of personal energy. This didn't mean I stopped being tactful or sensitive to the feelings of others; it only meant that I was more aware of when I was losing a sense of my own reality to those around me. It was like a little warning light flashing, telling me to stop and reassess my life.

Chapter Ten

My Secret Garden

At school we were often drawn into heated discussions about our individual religious and spiritual feelings. Yet the policy was to avoid professing any dogma or ideology that could create barriers. I found this a great relief, since the last thing I wanted was to become a member of a specific sect or religious group.

There was a consensus that one person's pudding could be another's poison, so very little judgment passed concerning the world view of others. Rather than dissipating energy through judgment and defensiveness, I was able to conserve my energy and use it to get in closer touch with my own internal source of information. This also allowed my personal brand of spirituality to grow stronger than ever.

"The beauty of being different from one another is like the beauty of a botanical garden," Anne explained one day. "Have you ever seen an oak trying to convince an evergreen to shed its leaves?"

Anne's comment made me think of my household: my Irish friends had been raised Catholic, while I had been brought up Presbyterian. Although none of us went to church anymore, there was definitely a religious attitude in our house. Unfortunately, this attitude rarely made us feel loved, happy, or wise. On the contrary, it seemed to make us more judgmental, inadequate, and guilt ridden.

While daydreaming about my household, I hadn't noticed that the day's meditation had already begun.

". . . And imagine you both *have* and *are* a secret garden. It grows by itself, but also needs nurturing by you, its invisible gardener. In the center of this garden is an enormous tree representing the center of your physical being. Experience the roots running deep into the ground, connecting you power, fully with the earth. Feel the trunk of your tree and all the many branches with green leaves. Feel how strong, grounded, and safe you can be as a tree."

I don't know if it was my strong affinity with trees, or whether I was in a particularly receptive state of mind this particular day, but the guided imagery worked so well I could feel tree bark against my skin.

"As you experience yourself as a tree, feel the warm sunlight shining on your leaves and branches. Hear the sounds of nature. What kind of tree are you?

"As a tree in the middle of this sacred territory, make this garden yours. If it's tended with love and care, you'll witness an amazing quantity of new growth within it. It will bring forth fruits and blossom with every kind of life you care to imagine.

"At birth, you inherited the whole of this remarkable place without consciously realizing it, and its beauty has been taken for granted. When the garden is neglected, you start to sense the change. You may feel that something is wrong and wonder indignantly why nobody is taking care of this old garden that has begun to turn brown and wither.

"Unfortunately, this has happened because you forgot that you are the keeper of your garden. Its potential was probably never explained to you or brought to your conscious mind as fully as you needed. Now I am reminding you: go ahead and make this paradise entirely yours!"

These words reminded me of the wonderful experience I had in the grounding class when we were asked to picture the earth in a colorful way. I had imagined paradise then.

"Now, I'd like you to focus in the center of the tree again," the voice continued. "Look around and be aware of the life outside you as your tree and all its leaves and branches reach to the heavens. You are firmly planted in the earth, its strength running to the very tip of your branches. At the same time, the creative force from the heavens is breathing into every leaf. You are securely fixed to the earth, yet heaven beckons you to reach for the sky. Above you the sun is shining, large and radiant. Its golden light is your highest creative essence. It fills you and surrounds you with life and vitality.

"When night descends over your garden and the sun has moved away, you get a chance to rest. If you resist the dark, you may feel alone—lost in the universe or forgotten by the gods and goddesses. Yet realize that your darkness and depression are simply inviting you to see things from a different perspective. Acknowledge your dark side: it carries a force and power of its own, which, according to nature, must also be honored. Its true dimension must be felt, owned, and realized. Only then can the cold and negative side of you be at peace with itself, allowing you to get a good night's rest."

I had never looked at my mood swings this way. I had always thought that getting depressed was a bad thing, like an insult to my creator. But now I was seeing how lack of inspiration simply offers some time out to reconnoiter.

"Sunrise brings another radiant day. The first shimmer of dawn is heralded by the birds. The many parts of your existence pulse around you, inhaling the clear, open spaces in huge breaths. You now feel composed and clear. It's a gift for you to use and enjoy. May you always remember this."

There was a long silence as we stretched and adjusted our awareness to the reality of the classroom. Anne smiled at us optimistically.

"Welcome back," she said.

"I feel like I just returned from a long vacation," I said.

"Look how much time and money you saved," a fellow student laughed.

After standing and stretching, we had a lengthy discussion on how to combine the "letting-go, all-natural, no-effort" attitude with the "being-responsible, create-your-own-reality" concept.

"As human beings we always walk the fine line between trust and action, perception and purpose," Anne said. "In this meditation, you covered both aspects: being the tree that grows just by standing there, and being the gardener having to labor with spades and hoes. Creating the garden you really like requires both inner receptivity and outer activity. They belong together, just like the act of breathing in and out."

Again it struck me how much I still needed to learn about the practicality of metaphysical knowledge. Every day I was able to comprehend just a little bit more about what it means to be a spiritual being enjoying an earthly body.

Chapter Eleven

Clairvoyant Pictures

I had attended the readings for several months now, sitting alongside the center-chair reader. During this time, most of my efforts had been geared to neutralizing "can't do it" pictures and developing confidence in my intuition. I just couldn't convince myself that the pictures on a mock television screen in my mind had anything to do with reality. I felt ashamed to describe what I was seeing, fearing it was only idle fantasy.

Just as Jeannie had demonstrated with me at the fateful party that introduced me to the school, my teachers told me over and over, "Just close your eyes and tell me what you see." All well and good, I thought. A nice child's game, but what did this have to do with clairvoyance? I still believed that when I finally became clairvoyant, I would have all sorts of fantastic and amazing psychic perceptions.

My teacher told me to explode that particular picture. "When you start seeing your first clairvoyant pictures, you probably won't even know it!" she said. "Those clairvoyant pictures will look like any other pictures you're used to seeing in your mind. Remember, you've been clairvoyant all your life! You haven't recognized clairvoyant pictures yet because they were always combined with your personal and subjective pictures, in one big mosaic. By giving supervised readings, especially with the continual feedback of the person being read, you're going to learn how to differentiate the clairvoyant pictures from all the others."

Indeed, I would communicate basic information that I sensed and get immediate reactions from my subject. In this way, I would find out if I were on the right track. Our most important goal was to perceive and impart information that would give our subjects fresh, valuable perspectives on their lives. Sometimes I came up with impressive details about people and their past and present experiences. Other times I couldn't see anything at all.

I'll never forget the day I saw my first consciously acknowledged clairvoyant picture. I was in class reading a fellow student's chakras when I saw a clear image in her second chakra of a sexual assault. The picture shocked me. I thought that surely it was "just my imagination." Nevertheless, I decided to check it out.

"I'm not quite sure how to ask this," I said, "but, uh, have you ever been raped?"

"God, you can see that? Yes! It happened when I was eighteen. I've been working very hard on those pictures. I've been saying hello to them, neutralizing them, but it's so difficult!"

I was flabbergasted. The experience of actually seeing a clairvoyant picture was entirely different from what I had expected, mainly because it felt so normal and simple. It was almost disappointing! I suddenly realized how many clairvoyant pictures must have passed through my mind without my ever knowing it.

We talked in class about the uncomfortable situation created when subjects wanted to test our abilities and expected to hear precise details about their lives reeled off matter-of-factly by a "bona fide clairvoyant." We called it the "prove it" game and were warned to ignore it and focus on the most important theme: what information does the subject really need?

The school was attracting more people like me—people who had possessed latent psychic abilities all their lives but who hadn't done anything astounding with them yet. There were no Edgar Cayces or flamboyant psychic geniuses capable of amazing feats of precognition or psychometry. Yet I believed that in the near future, intuitive observations like we practiced would become commonplace and considered an indispensable part of health care for both mind and body. In fact, my school experiences convinced me that being able to perceive clairvoyantly was no more astounding than being a violin player.

I was beginning to see a great similarity between learning the conscious use of clairvoyance and learning to play a musical instrument. Both begin with the development of self-assurance and trust. When I first started playing the violin at age nine, I felt clumsy and unnatural. So it was with my first attempts to consciously develop my intuitive abilities. Eventually, both violin playing and clairvoyant reading felt more natural and comfortable. As with the learning of music, the process of learning clairvoyant reading was helping me develop a greater awareness of my body as well as my mind.

As I learned how to play scales accurately on my violin, I was impressed with how my fingers developed a certainty of their own. In learning to play the violin, I eventually grasped the techniques of position, fingering, bow movement, and other details. The thinking part of me didn't have to work as hard with these basic techniques because the feeling part had thoroughly taken over. Similarly, while giving intuitive readings, I was learning how to ground, clean out my aura, explode roses, stay neutral, and so on. Eventually, I didn't have to think about these basic techniques; I could find the physical feeling in my body just by putting my attention on it.

At the school, we were told that both musicians and psychic readers may find themselves being pure channels for universal or cosmic forces: the personality can be transcended and the ego forgotten in the expression of some primary universal message. This was something we could hope for but not consciously strive for—something that would now and again, just happen.

Each reader at the school was encouraged to express his or her unique style. I began to notice how certain advanced readers were able to discern various aspects of complex patterns and communicate this effectively. I knew what it felt like to do this musically, and I longed for the day when I could do it with my readings.

Chapter Twelve

Center Chair

"Linda, I'd like you to be center chair tonight and read the chakras please," Kitty told me one night. A thousand thoughts raced through my head. What if I don't see anything? Am I capable of leading this reading? What if the subject doesn't agree with what I see?

After the other assignments were given, we went to the reading room, took our seats, and prepared to go into trance. I remembered that the most important thing was to stay calm and not worry. First we reviewed the procedure for getting into the proper frame of mind, along with the necessary checks and balances. Then we asked for guidance and the clarity to be pure and perceptive channels. "May light and love be my guide," I prayed nervously.

I felt my heart opening. I did a grounding exercise, feeling the earth energy flowing through my feet and legs and into the earth again. After grounding myself, I began "running energy" by visualizing not only the grounding, but cosmic and earth energy running up and down through my spinal column. By doing this, I felt a new base of strength and neutrality. Then I imagined roses around my aura to protect me from possible confusion when tuning into another person's abstract layers of being. I silently said my name a couple of times and experienced myself being wholly in my body in the here and now.

As I performed these exercises, I cleaned my aura

and chakras through visualization. When I came across haphazard mental pictures sitting idly on the movie screen of my inner eye, I blanked out that screen and prepared it to receive new pictures and information. If I saw pictures of fear or uncertainty, I exploded them in a rose, replacing them with the vibration of my golden sun.

I felt myself going into neutral, and the image of myself being a body of glass came to mind. I imagined information coming from the person I was reading flowing through me, having no effect on the resonance established by the readers as a whole.

The two other readers and I synchronized our energy by visualizing a golden vibration among us. The color gold, if visualized clearly, would raise our energy as a group to an extremely high level. It would allow us to clean out extraneous pictures and clear our channels of perception. As every color has its own vibration, color matching is the most direct way for a group to share information. We would often see the same mental pictures coming from the subject, or, as one mind, receive general intuitive information about this person.

About fifteen minutes passed. During this time the control walked around the room, helping us focus on the techniques. Her job was to be intuitively aware of everyone, including herself. This system had been devised to ensure the clarity and integrity of each reading.

Finally we were ready to start the reading. Our subject was an apprehensive young woman named Laurie, who was having a hard time sitting still in her chair. Despite her chaotic disposition, I felt strong and undistracted by her nervousness. I noticed that the atmosphere in the room was clear, strong, and well-grounded.

An important part of any reading is to communicate with the subject's being and—in our own minds—ask permission to proceed. It is important to ascertain whether the subject's inner self is ready to accept the information we might mirror back to it. With Laurie, we sought the appropriate timing for this, not wanting to interfere with her natural learning processes. We were not to say anything—no matter how correct we might be—that might cause a communication breakdown.

I pretended that my sixth chakra was an empty television screen ready to be turned on. I rubbed my palms together and held up my left hand. I asked my guides to help me see something on my television screen that related to my subject. Instantly I received images of panic, fear, and insecurity.

"It looks as if you're having difficulty feeling safe," I told Laurie. "Your first chakra is wide open, looking for information about survival. What's going on in your life that's causing you so much concern?"

"Well," the young woman answered, clearing her throat, "For starters, I'm afraid of losing my job, and my marriage is really in bad shape."

"I notice your heart chakra is closed. It's as if you can't bear to look at certain pictures concerning your fears about functioning well in the world."

I continued going through each chakra, explaining the function of each and how open or closed it was. This put a neutral atmosphere into the room, a mood of practicality.

I knew I was doing well that night. With others in the room following along, I felt secure knowing the trial-and-error process we were going through was safe. If one of us were to lose neutrality and objectivity by looking through his or her own pictures, we knew another reader would pick up on it.

"Good, Linda," the control whispered in my ear, "But don't forget to explode your matching pictures, eh?"

"Have I got so many?" I whispered back, surprised.

"Remember? You can have matching pictures without realizing it. Take time to look at them. It's good for you."

"Thanks," I mumbled. Indeed, I had many similar

pictures about feeling unsafe and insecure, although I felt very strong at the time. It was as if those pictures were just waiting to come out later, during a weaker state of mind. I decided not to let that happen and neutralized them before they could manifest themselves.

I continued reading Laurie's aura. "You're experiencing this chaotic period in your life because you need to make some basic changes. Your higher self wants to stir things up enough to make you want to grow further. On a higher level, you want more information about your abilities and how to better manifest yourself in the world.

"Also, you need to learn to appreciate your problems. They're more valuable than you realize. It's not always easy to admit, but our problems are our best friends."

For a moment, I felt as if I were Kitty or Bill.

"Why is that?" Laurie asked innocently.

"Because you always learn by solving them. Whether you know it or not, you chose life on this amazing planet in order to learn. So why not learn to love your difficulties right here and now?"

"But how can I love my problems and stay positive? I don't want to be like my mom. She loves her problems and creates more of them all the time—basically to attract attention and have an excuse to indulge in self-pity."

"Laurie," I said, "loving your problems the way we approach it here doesn't mean you should hold onto them. It means you allow them to be what they are. Make sure you aren't trying to escape a problem instead of trying to solve it. Often, resistance to a problem is the worst part of the problem! If you start to love your problems and say hello to them, this resistance will melt away. You transform a weakness into a strength."

As I said this, I was feeling like me again, not Bill or Kitty.

"Can you see what's going to happen in my marriage?" Laurie implored.

"I don't want to program your future," I answered her bluntly. "That's got to do with your own free will and the decisions you make when you come to them. What I want to offer you are possibilities and concepts you may or may not want to use or accept. You've got this reading on tape, now give yourself plenty of time to work with it. If you like, though, I'll take a look at the connections between the chakras of both you and your husband and describe the dynamics at work there."

Although Laurie's partner wasn't in the room, I could still "see" his connections with her. Through these mental pictures, I examined the relationship in terms of energy levels, receptivity, stuck patterns, and blockages on both sides. Later, Laurie told us that she could now look at her life with new insight and better face the work ahead of her. In turn, we readers noticed that her aura had taken on a light-golden hue, and that her grounding had improved immensely.

After neutralizing leftover matching pictures and making energy separations from Laurie and each other, we all met in the living room downstairs to share experiences. My success was celebrated. Once the news of my breakthrough had reached Kitty, she came over to me, grinning proudly, and said, "So, dear, how does it feel to be free?"

Chapter Thirteen

The Meaning of Color

After my successful reading with Laurie, I wanted to know more about colors and their profound meanings. Humankind has studied the metaphysical significance of color for thousands of years. Like astrologers, who ascribe meaning to the different formations of planets and stars, metaphysicians have assigned specific meanings to the various visible light frequencies we call colors. Yet, at our school, we weren't taught what any color *should* mean. Instead, we were asked to develop our own system of color interpretation through direct, personal experience. Free from worry about the interpretation of colors, we made up our own charts.

Interestingly enough, most of us students found ourselves in agreement about the meanings of the various basic colors. And we were in agreement, not only among ourselves, but often in relation to traditional metaphysical color interpretations.

As the days went on, we learned a great deal more about color—including the differences between inner-sight and outer-sight color interpretations, which Tom told us could be as different as night and day.

"They're not necessarily the same!" I remember him adamantly proclaiming in class. "Inner-sight versus outer-sight colors may have drastically different meanings, depending on the context in which they're found. For instance, if I see brown, black, gray, and dark green in a person's aura during a reading, I would assume he or she has some difficulties and negative experiences to work out. If I saw those same colors while walking in the woods, I wouldn't react to them in the same way. Those earthy hues would have a very positive influence on me. Furthermore, if I went out and bought a dark-blue suit, it wouldn't necessarily mean I was feeling depressed or sorry for myself! And a soft, gray wool sweater might give me a feeling of calm and relaxation, not boredom.

"Context, contrast, and texture can all change the meaning of color, and that's why any literal or simplistic approach to outer-sight color can be a difficult one," he concluded.

Based on my own perceptions during meditations and aura readings, I compiled the following list of inner-sight color interpretations. In addition to the colors described below in the following pages, there are many different hues and in between combinations of colors that need to be translated. During readings, I found I could use these either for general information or as powerful healing tools.

In the course of giving a reading, the colors we saw had to be clearly interpreted to communicate useful information to the subject. For this reason, we were taught to ask ourselves for meanings in the simplest terms. We received answers through our inner voices, usually through images on our sixth-chakra movie screens or through seventh-chakra knowing. We regularly used these information channels not only to interpret colors, but also to interpret all the pictures and symbols we received during a reading or meditation.

At the school, most readers worked more extensively with one particular system than another. Some got most of their information through symbols, others through colors. Some got most of their information through pictures, while others said they didn't see pictures at all but had a clear sense of knowing. Most of us specialized in one approach or another, whether visual, mental, abstract knowing, feeling, or hearing. It was up to each individual's tendencies and capabilities.

We also knew that during an aura reading there would often be a hodgepodge of information coming from the readers, because everyone had their own unique outlook. Kitty explained it well: "It's a mistake to believe that readers will see the very same things. They'll probably come up with strikingly similar conclusions," she said. "But how they get the information is an individual matter. Each reader will approach the subject from a slightly different angle and will see many different levels and qualities of information. This makes it much more challenging, of course! It also explains why often different readers see different colors while viewing the very same aura and imparting the same basic information. Remember, there are many paths to the top of the mountain."

Samples of Inner-Sight Color Interpretations

Shades of Black	Black: fear, negativity, foreign energy	Dark Gray: gloom, indifference, loss
	Gray: confusion, boredom, resignation	Silver (moon): versatility, power, astral travel
Shades of Brown	Dark Brown: stagnation, congestion, skepticism	Brown: groundedness
	Light Brown: earthiness	Copper: oneness with the earth
Shades of Red	Dark Red: hostility, injury, pain	Clear Red: passion, excitement
	Pinkish Red: creativity, enthusiasm, hope	Pink: love, affinity, forgiveness
Shades of Orange	Dark Orange: hidden emotions, mischievousness	Orange: creativity, forcefulness, humor
	Light Orange: spontaneity, vitality	Peach: nurturing, loving
Shades of Yellow	Mustard Yellow: cowardly, manipulative	Dark Yellow: intellectualizing, justifying
	Bright Yellow: wittiness, intellect, vigor	Light Yellow: wisdom, optimism, cheerfulness
Shades of Green	Dark Green: dishonesty, selfishness, jealousy	Forest Green: balance, growth

Samples of Inner-Sight Color Interpretations

	Light Green: healing, harmony, calm	Turquoise: strength, wisdom, playfulness
Shades of Blue	Dark Blue: repression, moodiness, solemnity	Royal Blue: royalty, adoration
	Sky Blue: clarity, confidence, expression	Silver Blue: confidence, trust
Shades of Indigo	Dark Indigo: dogmatism, repression	Clear Indigo: spiritual insight
	Purple: benevolence, knowledge	Light Purple: compassion, understanding
Shades of Violet	Dark Violet: spiritual dogmatism, repression	Lavender: self-respect
	Violet: self-knowledge, spiritual knowledge	Light Violet: high intent, spirituality
Shades of White	White: purity, innocence	Milky White: protection
	Transparent White: un-groundedness, unreality	
Shades of Gold	Whitish Gold: supremacy, protection (sun)	Yellowish gold: rejuvenation, absolute intelligence
	Pinkish Gold: absolute love, healing	

Chapter Fourteen

Gray-Colored Glasses

As summer approached, I decided I needed to get away from the school for a while and find a new equilibrium. It was part of the major "growth period" I had propelled myself into. I had heard this term innumerable times during my training. It was meant to describe the periods in our lives when practically nothing seems to be going right—or at least what we *think* is right.

At any rate, a communication gap had been steadily widening between me and the rest of my musical household. My Irish love had returned to his emerald isle, and I desperately needed some time to reassess my personal relationships. Consequently, I was considering living by myself. The thought both scared me and gave me a strange sense of exhilaration.

I had learned that these so-called growth periods occur when a person's newly expanded awareness raises the vibration of the life-force energy. This newly raised energy usually has a difficult time integrating with the physical body, thus creating all kinds of physical or emotional reactions.

It seemed that growth periods were being revealed in at least one student in our circle on a regular basis. Typical statements describing various growing pains would sound like this: "I feel out of control mentally and emotionally. I'm so depressed! I feel insecure and fearful. I become easily angry or indignant. I feel sorry for myself and wish I could blame others for my problems. I got clumsy and broke my favorite teapot! I feel absent-minded and unreal. I'm constantly tired."

As students, we had witnessed how emotional and spiritual growth spurts can be expressed in a number of ways—anger, fear, sorrow, and aggression being among the most common. We often dealt with these uncomfortable growth periods in an overtly jovial manner, knowing that humor was often the best remedy:

"Oh Jake? He's just in anger right now. I think he's finally pierced through his own thick skin." Or, "Yeah, Janet's been stuck on that picture for weeks now. It's her favorite one. She thinks everybody's against her."

This is not to say that we weren't loving or supportive of our fellow classmates. We had simply learned long ago that going into sympathy with someone would often prolong their agony. We knew that people would end up being the most grateful if left alone to solve their own problems.

We also noticed that everyone would ultimately come through their most nasty growth periods unscathed. After a person's negative thoughts had been owned and discharged, a delicious sensation of lightness, clarity, freedom, and self, confidence would usually emerge. It left the feeling that, in spite of all the complaints and unhappiness, the pain of growing had been worth it after all.

On one hand, I had learned so much so fast during my intuitive training that I felt positively transformed. On the other hand, I often saw myself as completely inadequate in making my life work out, and this threw me into an emotional upheaval. I felt how an angel might feel being forced to walk in a stiff pair of hiking boots. My spiritual feet were on the ground, hurting, while my soul wanted to fly above the clouds.

I had been disinterested in the other students lately

and didn't know why. I even felt out of harmony with the teaching staff. Their jokes didn't make me laugh anymore. For all the marvelous information I had acquired at this remarkable place, I found myself thinking it had become routine. Or was it me? I wasn't capable of answering questions like these at the time.

One would think I should have understood my problem better. Besides having witnessed many other people's growth periods during my training. I had also witnessed their anguish while "stuck on a picture," unable to stop their fixations. This is a common problem. Being stuck on a picture causes a temporary collapse in objectivity and movement: the person who's stuck is unable to neutralize the dominant picture, and it becomes blinding. In fact, the picture has such an emotional charge that it maintains control over that person's entire reality.

I knew I was looking at the school through gray-colored glasses, yet I felt like keeping those glasses on my nose for a while. I would do whatever I liked! I made the decision to stop attending the school for the entire summer. And I hadn't been very polite about it: for the first time in my life I had been openly angry and didn't feel guilty. No one else at the school seemed startled by my different behavior. I believe many of them thought it was long overdue.

We had heard much about our need to embrace the negative aspects of our personalities. I was obviously identifying with that need. I realized that all my life I'd had the terrible habit of trying to please others at my own expense. The thought of hurting other people's feelings or wondering what other people might think about me was terrifying. All the months of soul searching at the school brought this out very clearly, and I finally saw how much energy and inner focus I had lost all my life because of it.

By the end of the summer; after a successful vacation at a music camp, I had happily removed and discarded my gray-colored glasses. My rebellious attitude toward the school had dwindled to insignificance. I even felt homesick for the place and prayed they would take me back.

On my return, I was relieved to be greeted kindly and found that no one judged me for my absence. I was shocked to discover, however, that most of my fellow classmates had grown tremendously. Students I had earlier considered slow or totally stuck were now reading center chair! Finding such big changes among my classmates was humbling. I felt I must do some serious hustling now, to catch up and find a new sense of confidence.

Chapter Fifteen

Not Alone

As a child, I used to wriggle beneath the covers to the foot of my bed with my younger brother to look for "Mousey." This invisible creature was my brother's imaginary friend, always around somewhere, ready to help out. When either of us got into trouble, Mousey was usually to blame. Mousey became convincingly real to me, and I believe he must still exist somewhere as a tiny guardian spirit for some little person.

As I grew up, I became increasingly aware of the loving beings surrounding me. Sometimes at night I would look at my bedroom wall and stare at the shadows cast from the streetlight outside. I would talk with my "shadow people" about awesome, fantastic things that would often cause me to get goose bumps or tears in my eyes.

After the death of my grandmother; I had the distinct sensation of being watched over. I felt she still existed somewhere, in some other dimension. As an adult, it became obvious to me that all humans are constantly watched over and helped by intangible beings.

In class, we were regularly given guided fantasies to help us contact our personal guardians. Sometimes I got clear pictures of what they looked like, but more often it was simply the awareness of a presence.

One day at school, I discovered three new guides whose presence was much more real than I was accustomed to. For several weeks I was terribly preoccupied, thinking about them almost all the time, giving them names and wondering what they had to tell me next. One morning, I awoke with an irritated feeling and didn't know why. As I lay in bed thinking about it, I realized that my friendship with these new guardians had gone too far. I felt I was being watched over night and day, that I had lost all my privacy, although I knew these beings were there to help me. This could be likened to making friendships in the physical world and allowing the relationships to develop too intensely and too fast. It reminded me of the way I've often felt in restaurants when the waiters come around too often asking if everything is OK. "There are limits to everything," I said out loud. "Even to spiritual relationships!"

This experience made me very aware of how I needed to focus more on myself, within my personal earthly setting. Now I understood why my guardians had always been so vague before. They weren't supposed to distract me or take away my privacy. They were supposed to keep a low profile, allowing me private experiences on earth.

I thanked my new spirit friends for the experience of having them so present and then watched them recede into the background of my conscious mind. I knew they would be there when I really needed them. I knew that somehow they would continue communicating with me through intuition, impulsive actions, and dreams, making their presence more obvious when necessary.

When giving aura readings, I made a point of checking my subjects' relationships with their guides. I looked to see if their guides were allowing the subjects enough freedom and ownership of their private psychic territory. We defined a "positive" guide as one who helped a person trust himself more. A "negative" guide was one who tried to control a person and take away her psychic freedom and authority. Just like human relationships, we all need to know who our true friends are and how they are affecting us.

Even loving and helpful guides don't need to occupy our psychic boundaries, except temporarily when we are learning directly from them; or when we are sick, in danger, or emotionally distressed.

Our school had a good rule of thumb for anyone who had a conscious rapport with his or her spiritual helpers: no spiritual guardian has any superiority over a being in a physical body. General misunderstanding about this point throughout history has resulted in people being "possessed" by entities, with the helpless victims taken over, tortured, or even destroyed by dark spiritual forces.

Over and over again, I heard at school that any physical being is always "senior" in his or her psychic territory. This means that on earth, a physical being is many times more powerful than any spiritual entity by virtue of being human and having physical substance. The horror of possession can be completely overcome merely by grounding the physical body, having the victim release all fear, and telling the spirit to go away. It's that simple. Essentially, the problem of possession lies in the "victim's" inability to realize his or her personal power and freedom.

We were taught that inside each of us is all the wisdom we will ever need. This wisdom, available to us via our intuitive selves, can be contacted via the image of the "inner teacher." Before meeting our inner teacher, we were guided in meditation to discover our own private "sanctuary." A person's sanctuary is a place of total peace, safety, and creative resourcefulness. Through guided fantasy, we roamed our inner world and sought out this very special, personal place—a place we could go anytime we wished, just by thinking about it.

Usually, a person's sanctuary is found somewhere in nature—in a sunny meadow, in the forest, at the seashore, on top of a mountain, in a shady glen—wherever the world seems perfect and beautiful. I was exhilarated by vivid accounts other students gave about their special places of power and joy. It convinced me, more than ever, of the validity and power of each person's creative imagination.

After we became familiar and comfortable with our own sanctuary, we were ready to meet with our inner teacher. He or she would appear somewhere along a pathway leading toward the sanctuary. An inner teacher could reveal him or herself in an unlimited variety of forms. One student might meet a bearded old man in sandals and a long white robe, another an exotic princess, still another a businessman dressed in a suit and tie and carrying a briefcase. I'll never forget a class of Tom's in which one man perceived his inner teacher to be a buxom, mini-skirted disco dancer.

"By God," he exclaimed, "this is going to be more fun than I thought!"

"My inner teacher was Jesus," a woman said. "I've never felt this peaceful in my life."

"We all have the Christ within us," Tom answered kindly. "That's a beautiful way of discovering it."

"My inner teacher was just a presence, like a lovely, glowing golden-pink light," said one man. "There was so much love coming from this presence! I can't possibly describe it." He lapsed into heaving sobs and was given a comforting hug by the woman next to him.

It was fascinating to hear about each other's experiences, yet it was customary to keep much of our information to ourselves. Talking too much about our personal experiences could sometimes interfere with the deeper process of integration and understanding. The continuous interaction with our inner teachers contributed tremendously to our spiritual growth and insight. It also made us increasingly aware of the vast potential within us, just waiting to be tapped and utilized.

Chapter Sixteen

Past Lives

In the course of many readings given by myself and others at the school, I discovered that the most common negative life theme is for human beings to dislike themselves. This phenomenon creates unhappy and self-perpetuating experiences that are repeated over and over. Dislike of self has probably been the most powerful instrument of misery and suffering on earth. To become free from our deep-rooted, self-abusive patterns, we need to view them with fresh, positive understanding.

As I gained more experience as a reader, I could clearly observe how the dislike of self is related to our past-life experiences. When I first started reading, I found it difficult to sensitively incorporate any past-life information into the rest of the reading. Being unable to prove the validity of any past-life information I uncovered frequently caused my confidence to plunge. Discussion of a past life would seem fruitless when my subjects had no recollection of it themselves. It was like trying to argue the existence of dreams with someone who has never remembered having any. In this case, my solution was to translate past-life images into information that would help the person better understand their present life's situation.

In general, unless there was some specific, guided purpose, journeying into past lives was not recommended at the school because of the great emphasis placed on the here and now. I learned to mention a person's past lives only if those pictures were strongly lit up in their aura, or if a specific past life was showing its direct relevance to the subject's current problems. As opposed to present-life impressions, these past-life pictures emanated an entirely different quality, something akin to an old, black-and-white movie being played next to Technicolor.

The more I looked into other people's past lives, the more I realized how I was carrying around some very emotionally charged past-life pictures of my own. It became apparent to me, through my own meditations and through the help of other readers, that a large chunk of my life-force energy was stuck in the past. This made it very difficult for me to be grounded in the present. Since my childhood days, I had enjoyed the dreamy, mystical qualities associated with ungroundedness. But unfortunately, it had often left me feeling lost and surrounded by chaos.

At any rate, there was this "other me" I had discovered from a recent past life. I had seen her periodically during meditations. Often she presented a huge problem for me because I would become obsessed by pictures of her traumatic death. It was obvious that much of my life-force energy was entangled in that experience, surrounded by deep fear.

I was instructed by other readers to first say hello to all the pictures and emotions associated with that death experience—including a recurring nightmare from childhood—in order to "own" those experiences more completely. "Owning" something means being able to face it, for you can only solve a problem if you are able to admit you've got it.

After owning those past-life pictures, I was taught to gather them with my thoughts, place them in an imaginary rose, and explode the rose. I was taught to practice this exercise until I felt at peace with the pictures that had upset me. As I repeated this neutralizing process and visualized bright sunlight radiating above my head and streaming into my body, I consciously took my energy out of the past and came more and more into the present moment. As the pictures became increasingly neutralized, it was as if I had dropped a very heavy load. I thought less and less of that "other me" and even began to joke about her. On a daily basis, I watched myself become stronger, more real, and definitely more capable.

Anne offered our group a powerful image to help us integrate our experiences, either past or present: "Imagine time as a circle. Imagine this circle as the rim of a large wheel. Your wholeness—your entire beingness—and highest creative essence is the hub of this wheel. Many spokes radiate from the hub, and each spoke is a different lifetime, representing a different personality and a different aspect of your total being. When focusing on one particular spoke in the physical realm, while living it, all the other realms are nearly forgotten in the constant exercise of that oddity called free will.

"Having your consciousness expand the physical body, as in meditation, dreams, or after death, is going back to the center of the wheel, where there awaits an undeniable point of wholeness to your being, an undeniable *place to be*, containing all the wisdom any personality could ever need.

"Whatever a personality learns in the physical world is carried through each life, each spoke of the wheel, into that beingness in the center—the eternal part of you that never ceases to grow in wisdom, knowledge, and experience."

I knew that the eternal part of me, found in the center of this miraculous wheel, was my own soul, or higher self. I knew that, in gaining perspective about dilemmas that have persisted, perhaps through lifetimes, human beings will eventually learn to forgive themselves. In this way, they will become capable of ending many lifetimes of painful and self-destructive themes.

Chapter Seventeen

Graduation

As graduation approached and our group of twelve neared the end of its magical journey, I stood back, astonished.

"Linda, if it weren't for all your wonderful freckles, I'd think you were a different person than the student I met two years ago," Kitty told me, laughing. "You've been one of the least confident yet most capable students I've ever worked with. You survived this place! Congratulations."

Confidence had been a central issue for everyone. There seemed to be two kinds of student: those who were perpetually unsure and those who were too sure. Both were incomplete. Both had to confront their egos. Everyone faced a constant struggle, trying to find the right balance between certainty and uncertainty. The more knowledge we summoned via intuition, and the more often we used it to serve others, the more important it was for us to remember that we were to be messengers for the Light, to strive for the highest good for all, and to be grateful rather than proud of our intuitive skills.

Occasionally, some readers would forget and become proud anyway. Fortunately, fellow students served as terrific watchdogs. "Be careful, Sue, don't trip over your robes..." might be a typical reminder.

Then there was Bill's classic story about the boy who was trying to help his father carry a heavy log through the woods. When the job was done, the boy looked up at his father with pride and said, "See how strong I am?" Bill liked to use this story when one of us forgot that everything we do and accomplish comes from a divine source. We weren't allowed much space for ego-tripping when it came to helping and healing, simply because the two activities aren't compatible.

One woman in our group, despite all her diligence, was not allowed to graduate. She was somewhat deficient in discipline and often fell into a tailspin, getting confused about her true purpose in life. There was a lack of clear intent behind her outpouring of enthusiasm, reflecting a lost connection with the Great Spirit Her teachers and classmates had supported her unconditionally, yet strangely it was difficult for her to clearly define her goals. It was as if she were stuck in a never-ending growth period. Years later, I heard she had become a successful dancer. Apparently this had been her saving grace. The power of pure physical expression had enabled her to connect more naturally with the Source. It had rescued her from the addictive mind trips that made her life so frustrating.

Those of us who did graduate certainly knew we weren't perfect beings. But we felt competent enough to function productively in the demanding outside world. Having taken authority over our lives, we knew it was possible to live in trust rather than fear, soaring like eagles above the plains of our lives.

All my life, I have found it interesting that the American national bird is the bald eagle. According to Native American mythology, "eagle medicine" is the power of the divine, our connection to the Great Spirit. The bald eagle symbolizes our chance to soar to great heights of inspiration while remaining well grounded in the earthly realms. It represents our ability to see the larger patterns of life and to keep them in mind when experiencing difficulties. For many Native American tribes, the eagle symbolizes a state of grace achieved through hard work, compassion, and the successful resolution of life's trials and tribulations. This offers the chance to own one's personal power because the highs and lows of earthly existence have been met and accepted.

Graduation day was approaching. Like everyone else, I was preparing to let go. I was preparing to leave this unusual place and all the good-hearted people I had come to love. It wasn't easy. I felt like a downy eaglet getting ready to fly.

PART TWO

INTUITION MAGIC WORKSHOP

Chapter One

Developing Perceptive Imagination

Every human being is born with the miraculous tools of clairvoyance. The word *clairvoyant* means simply "clear seeing." Interestingly, the way people have come to use the term acknowledges that it is not our eyes that are the tools for this "clear seeing." Rather, our power for this visual clarity comes from an inner sight, or "sixth sense." That sixth sense provides us with understandings about the world that cannot be registered with our eyes or the rest of our five outer senses.

Natural clairvoyance is the survival tool that infants use to make decisions before they learn language or the meaning of people's actions. Because clairvoyance is linked with our imagination, most of us begin to ignore clairvoyant messages in the course of growing up. We are taught that information from our imagination is arbitrary, not based on the "real world," and of little practical value. We are conditioned to believe that what we see in our mind's eye is so whimsical and haphazard that it doesn't really matter what goes on there, as long as it doesn't interfere with "actual reality" or "normal functioning." Because of this attitude, we cripple one of the most reliable and natural sources of information and creativity within us.

Many of us have forgotten how to use our imagination. As children, you employed it to bring joy, adventure, and intuitive wisdom into your life. However, Western society's emphasis on the concrete outer world has likely undermined your ability to visualize and imagine, thus unconsciously restricting your capacity to be naturally creative and to solve problems through intuition. Fortunately, however, intuition can be reawakened and strengthened through practice.

Intuition is knowing without reasoning. It's sensing information coming from your own source within, without intellectual effort. How thoroughly and effectively you develop and use your intuition will depend on your personal interest, attitude, and conditioning. You will need to cultivate self-trust while clearing and strengthening the lines of communication between your inner and outer worlds.

Most of the exercises in the Intuition Magic Workshop will help you unblock or widen the channels of communication that facilitate inner sight and intuitive wisdom. Visualize yourself becoming a finely tuned instrument, capable of discerning many subtle levels of information that until now you have habitually ignored.

When learning how to perceive clearly with your inner sight, it makes no difference where you start. The vital factor is whether you will allow yourself to reclaim your forgotten ability. Just like developing any artistic talent, it's important that you be patient and have confidence in your latent abilities while giving yourself time to let the learning take hold. The effective use of your inner sight will grow according to the rate your entire psychological system can handle and incorporate it. Trust the process!

The following exercises will help you strengthen your inner sight. To begin, simply give yourself permission to "see" from this inner perspective. You may visualize with your eyes closed, or while staring at a fixed point, or even while reading this book. It's important to mention that some people are less oriented toward their inner sight than they are toward their intuitive feelings and a sense of knowing.

If this is the case for you, try doing these exercises more on a feeling level and less on a vivid picture-making level.

Try variations, make adjustments for yourself, and keep in mind that each person has his or her own way of effectively using the imagination. The important thing is to direct your attention toward becoming better focused, without being scattered, and with more confidence than you may be accustomed to. Practice as few or as many of the exercises as you like, and create your own tempo of learning.

The Center of Your Head

Make yourself comfortable and imagine going to the center of your head, focusing your mind on the area behind your eyes and between your ears. This is a crucial location—it is your "home base," in a sense, the place where you can learn to relax and consciously develop your intuitive and clairvoyant abilities. Getting in touch with the center of your head is like finding a good seat in a private movie theater. You need to be properly situated to clearly see the insightful films projected onto the personal screen of your mind.

If you find it difficult to center yourself this way, imagine seeing the back of your eyeballs in front of you, your nose from within, and your ears on both sides. Listening to inner physical sounds (like your breathing, your heartbeat, or the blood running next to your eardrums), will help you to get into the center of your head.

While you're doing this, you will no doubt find that your attention loves to wander. Sounds around you may tempt your attention to go elsewhere. Or you may find yourself thinking of what you should do after the exercise is over, focusing on the future instead of being in the center of your head in the present moment. Don't judge yourself if this happens! Most people, accustomed to having their attention roam like a stray animal, have a hard time staying focused for more than a few seconds. When your attention roams, gently pull it back inside your head.

This exercise can be used as a basic form of meditation. It will help you develop your power of concentration. It is also the important first step in preparing you to accurately perceive intuitive and clairvoyant information.

The Analyzer

Part of our brain always wants to analyze, control, and explain everything. Kitty and Bill called this part of ourselves "the analyzer." People who identify strongly with the analyzer may find it difficult to feel and understand their intuitive wisdom because they are always looking for rational explanations.

If you can maintain well-focused attention in the center of your head, you can experience a neutral state of mind in which intuitive and clairvoyant information can flow. However, the analyzer can clog this peaceful setup if you let it, so you must learn to do something about it.

Go inside your head and imagine that your analyzer emits a tone based on its activity. The more active and controlling your analyzer is, the higher the frequency it generates. What frequency do you hear inside your head? Hum the tone out loud.

Now imagine a little knob in the center of your head that regulates the activity of your analyzer. Turn it down and hear the tone frequency going down. Play with this knob until you find a tone that makes you feel comfortable.

If this technique doesn't work right away, simply ignore your thinking self in a loving way. Just as you can hike alongside a freeway with your own pleasant thoughts, you can learn to ignore all the thought congestion rushing inside you. As you do this, you will more easily be able to discern valuable messages that transcend rational explanations— messages that put you on the path toward inner peace and knowledge.

Colors

Opening yourself to the idea of perceiving colors in your mind is a very good way to stimulate clairvoyant ability. Imagine all the colors you can think of, one at a time. Realize that imagination can be any inner experience: a distinct feeling, a clear thought, an inner word. Don't be intimidated by the terms *imagination* and *visualization*. A perception doesn't have to be visual in order to be real. Feeling or auditory perceptions are just as valuable, even in relation to colors.

Exploding Roses

To develop your perceptive imagination, you need to acknowledge the fact that you are capable of creating or dissolving any mental image. The following exercise is useful because it represents the balance between consciously creating an image and consciously letting go of it. This process of letting go can be difficult, yet just as you are able to create with your mind's eye, you can also learn to "uncreate" with it. The processes ignited in the brain by practicing this are essential for owning the power you really have to govern your life.

Imagine a large red rose in front of you displaying all the details you can think of: stem, leaves, thorns, dew on its petals, etc. To have a clearer image to work with, you might want to look at a real rose or find a good photograph and study it. Try all colors and types of roses and see how real you can make them. Also, smell the rose and imagine what it feels like to touch a petal, a leaf, or a thorn.

Now picture one of your beautiful roses and allow it to disappear into thin air. You can do this by imagining a tiny explosion, or by simply allowing the rose to fade away quickly. Whichever way you make your rose disappear, it helps to do it quickly and with no regrets! Unlike the physical level, the mind allows you to create and uncreate without pain or effort. See if you're able to develop a sense of objectivity about the process of watching your images come and go.

Looking at Another Person

Have a friend sit in a chair about four feet away from you, hands apart and feet flat on the floor. With your physical eyes, take a good look at your friend, noticing the clothes and colors and fine details. Now close your eyes and recapture the same image in your mind.

Next, from the center of your head with eyes closed, look for any colors that may show up around your friend's body. Look specifically at the head and shoulders, chest, arms, hands, waist, legs, and feet. If you see any colors around these areas, say them aloud to your friend. When you're finished, while still in the center of your head, say your name to yourself three times.

Chapter Two

Acknowledging Earth and Body

Many spiritual traditions cast aspersions on the body—along with the earth in general—referring to it as a trap, a prison, an illusion, or even the root of all evil. I take a more optimistic perspective. I find it constructive to view the body as a great temple that houses our spirit, as well as a miraculous and necessary tool for the success of our soul's great journey. Our bodies provide constant challenges to stimulate learning and growth. Look at your body with a smile and say: "This is the body I am now creating as my very own vehicle for my soul's purpose." The following exercises may help you learn to enjoy your body more and tune in to earthly wisdom.

Grounding

When people say that someone appears "spaced out" or "not all here today," they are really referring to a person's grounding. Being well-grounded means having a reference point on earth where you can tap into the natural flow of earth energy. Being well-grounded helps you deal with matters on the physical, earthly plane of existence. Unless you are well-grounded, many of your ideas and creative forces will languish as idle dreams and unmanifested visions. You may be a highly gifted or talented person, but without grounding, you may be unable to do anything with those gifts and talents.

If you feel yourself only marginally grounded, don't despair. You're not the only one. Lack of solid grounding is more common than the common cold or the flu!

Being ungrounded can be due to painful earthly experiences that have left you unwilling to accept some of the physical-plane responsibilities that come with occupying a body. Unwittingly, ungrounded people tend to project their consciousness away from their bodies to other psychic levels where the physical body isn't needed. The physical body then suffers from minimum maintenance, which creates a subconscious level of bodily distress that often manifests as feeling unsafe or fearful. However, through proper grounding you can connect your body with the earth and create a complete circuit of earth energy, increasing your feelings of safety and protection. Grounding is surrendering yourself to the planet's gravity, which is one of the most natural things a person can do.

Here is an easy technique for grounding yourself: Sit in a chair with your feet flat on the floor. Visualize the soles of your feet absorbing earth energy, feeling it flow up your legs to your thighs and into the base of your spine. Sense the area at the base of your spine as a tingling ball of earth-fed energy.

After you have done this, imagine you're growing golden roots at the base of your spine—golden roots that drop down into the earth. This is your grounding cord. You are free to imagine your grounding cord to be made of anything you like—a laser beam, a golden chain, a cable, a rope, a tube, a concrete pole, or any other symbolic form. Let yourself imagine the kind of grounding cord that best suits your needs.

Allow your grounding cord to sink deep into the earth, traveling through all the layers of our planet to finally reach the center. Allow your cord to fuse with earth's radiant, sun, like center, giving your body a solid and constant attachment to the planet. You now have a beautiful energy connection from the base of your spine to the center of the earth.

Now make your grounding cord twice as wide and feel the difference. Then mentally double its width again. Now let it go back to its original width. Then make it twice as narrow. How does this feel? Make it twice as narrow again and notice the difference. Finally, choose the kind of grounding that feels the best at this moment and allow yourself to experience it fully.

Next, change the color of your grounding cord and feel the difference that makes. Pick the color that feels right for now. If you're not sure what color to choose, ask your body to tell you. Don't analyze; just accept what comes to mind first.

To complete this grounding exercise, allow the earth energy to flow up through your feet, up your legs, into the base of your spine, and then back down your grounding cord into the earth. Without effort, simply allow this to happen, even if you don't experience a physical sensation at first.

Another playful and effective grounding technique is to pretend you are a tree. Again, sit comfortably in a chair with your feet flat on the floor. Imagine you are a very large and sturdy tree with roots running deep into the earth. Feel the earth energy bubbling into your feet and legs. The trunk of your tree also connects your tailbone, in a straight line, to your roots. Allow any tension or excess energy to run into the ground through these roots.

This tree visualization can be especially beneficial for people suffering from physical ailments of the feet, legs, or lower body zone. If you're feeling particularly unsafe, dizzy, or "out of the body," it's wise to ground your entire body and aura by imagining earth energy resonating around you and within you. Visualize that you are connected like a powerful shaft to the center of the earth.

People who have trouble with their grounding may also find dance, sports, or martial arts very helpful in making this important energy connection from body to earth.

Talking to the Earth

Grounding not only establishes a direct means of receiving energy from the earth, it also creates a foundation for developing a personal communication with the spirit of the earth. It is this spirit that people intuitively refer to when they speak of "Mother Earth." Superficially, it may appear that the earth is a soulless platform to which biological life has attached itself, in the same manner that a petri dish is the sterile platform to which laboratory biology experiments are attached. But in reality, our entire Planet Earth is a conscious, living, growing entity, alive with atoms and molecules and energies we have yet to fully comprehend.

Being able to communicate with the earth is as important as being able to communicate with your friends and family: it is essential to health and happiness. You may ask, "How can I possibly communicate with the earth?"

First of all, be open to the idea. Allow yourself to be excited with the deep desire to talk with an old friend. Via your grounding cord, send a "hello" into the earth. Inside yourself, say "Hello, Earth," then wait. Continue doing this until you feel you are being heard and that the earth is ready to acknowledge your greetings. Wait to see what kind of reaction you get. It doesn't have to be a vision or an "earth-shaking" experience, although it might be. It might be quiet words or tender feelings welling up inside. It might also be a memory or a symbol.

Going further with your dialogue, imagine you are going to give Mother Earth a present. This can be anything—whatever comes to mind. Send this present down your grounding cord. See, hear, feel, sense, or know that it is being accepted, then imagine the earth giving you a present in return. Allow the symbol, feeling, or picture you receive to settle somewhere in your body or in your aura.

You might find yourself having problems grounding or not feel in the mood to connect with the earth. But you still need it! As children of the earth, our grounding with our home planet is like a lifelong umbilical cord that feeds us and makes us safe. When you are fearful or despairing, ask the earth to send you the grounding cord you need so badly. Ask and ye shall receive.

Remember, the earth is a loving spirit; it has no dutiful expectations of you. If the communication you get from the earth is not loving, realize that your perception might be blurred by your own negative attitudes. You might need to reassess your relationship with our precious mother planet.

Body Talk

Think of the body as your lifelong, inseparable companion and realize the value of being on friendly terms with it. Your body contains tremendous wisdom. By silently talking to your body, you can easily summon intuitive information from it. There are so many conflicting ideas these days about what is good and not good for our bodies. But what does your own body have to say about it? You can find out more easily than you realize.

Sometimes your body understands your needs much better than your rational mind. For instance, you can ask your stomach what it wants to eat for dinner when your mind doesn't have a clue. If you want to take a walk and are in a quandary over where to go, you can ask your legs to carry you to the right place. There are endless possibilities to discover and experience when it comes to "body talk."

Before you start talking to your body, though, there

are a few things you can do to make it more attentive. As you sit on your chair, stamp your feet on the floor, rub your hands over your thighs, feel your face and your head, lay your hands to rest on your heart and stomach. Stretch if you like.

Now sit comfortably in your chair and be in the center of your head. Check the "tone frequency" of your analyzer. If necessary, turn it down a little. Remember, you want to be talking to your body, not just your rational mind.

Now greet your body and tell it that you love it. Thank it for all the wonderful things it does for you without having to be asked. Then start asking your body questions and be ready to see, hear, feel, or otherwise know the answers inside yourself.

What does your body feel about your diet? Is it getting all the essential nutrients it needs? Do you drink enough liquids—especially, pure water? Do the foods you eat make your body feel good? Are there some foods your body needs that you haven't been giving it? Ask what these foods are.

Have no judgments about whether these foods are supposedly healthy or unhealthy. Your body has a wisdom of its own; it may need the *feeling* associated with a particular food rather than the food itself. For instance, a certain food may help you to get in touch with a happy memory.

Here are some more questions: Does your body need any specific vitamins or minerals? Does it feel like eating more or less? Does it feel like going to a doctor or naturopath? Are you allowing your body to breathe in an optimal way? Is your breathing shallow or deep? Is it relaxed or forced and tight? Do you sometimes forget to breathe?

How does your body like the way you stand and move? Does it feel free enough? Does it like to dance or participate in sports? If so, what kind? Are there any special kinds of movements your body would like to make? Does your body get to communicate enough with other bodies?

Does your body get enough rest and sleep? How

does your body like your pace of life? Does it need more regularity or more variation? How does your body feel in general? Ask it what it wants and needs to be happy.

Now bend over and drop your head between your knees, allowing any tensions in your back, shoulders, arms, hands, neck, and head to flow into the earth. Sit up slowly and thank your body for the great conversation.

It's important to realize that this talk you just had with your body is providing answers for the here and now. For instance, if your body just told you it wanted a candy bar, it doesn't mean you should eat one every day. Maybe your body just wants a taste and not the whole bar. Every moment is unique, and so are your body's needs and wants. Take more time to create a loving and intimate rapport with your body. Your entire being may be very pleased with the results.

Chapter Three

Out-of-Body Perspectives

As much joy as the body provides, it is useful to leave this physical base once in a while to look at life from a more abstract level. Whether we remember it or not, we do this every night when we dream.

Leaving the body is a quick and efficient way of seeing yourself more objectively. It often takes only a bit of distance from a problem to be able to put it into better perspective. If you find yourself in a bad mood or bogged down for any reason, take a look at yourself from a distance. This more expansive view is often useful for getting "unbogged" and out of that bad mood. Following are some valuable exercises.

Looking at Yourself

Sit comfortably in a chair with your hands apart and your feet flat on the floor. Find a corner of the room above you, not too far away. Take a good look at what it's like and where it is in relation to you. Now close your eyes and imagine you are sitting in that corner looking down at yourself in the chair. Make it real.

Try this for a moment, then shift your attention back to the center of your head as you sit in your chair. Now shift back again to the corner, looking down, observing the clothes you're wearing, the way you're sitting, what your face and hair look like, etc. Notice colors and details. Practice going back and forth, and make it as clear and real as you can. If being outside your body makes you feel afraid, create a silver cord of light from the crown of your head that clearly connects you to your body below.

Another viewpoint you can use is that of a bird hovering above yourself and looking down. Or, if you're nervous about flying or don't like heights, simply visualize yourself sitting in a chair opposite yourself. After you've finished the exercise and returned to your body, always be in the center of your head and clearly feel your grounding cord again for several minutes before resuming other activities.

Some people find it difficult or even frightening to focus their attention from outside their body. In such cases, it's good to remember that out-of-body attention is always connected with the body in a very elastic way. It's the same when you come back into your body after dreaming. If you're still not ready to experience these outside-yourself exercises, you can get a similarly objective viewpoint by imagining yourself in a mirror or visualizing a picture of yourself.

If none of these exercises work, ask yourself if you actually *do* want to face yourself. It might represent a major confrontation you're not yet prepared for. In any case, don't judge yourself. If the answer is no, that's fine. Maybe you'll want to do it some other time.

A Flying Exercise

Sit in a chair with your eyes closed and imagine that you've grown a beautiful set of wings. You are so happy with your wings that you feel like trying them out in your imagination. There is a large, open window right next to you. You know you can fly out the window and be totally free. On this warm, sunny day, you can fly anywhere you like and create any people, places, or activities you like—towns, oceans, rivers, forests, mountains, whatever. You can also create any sounds or music you want to hear, any fragrance you want to smell. Moreover, you can play any role you want to play, knowing that at any moment you can fly right back to your open window and back to the chair where you started.

When you finish this exercise, remove your wings and focus your entire attention in the center of your head. Visualize your grounding cord again for several minutes and say your name out loud. Say the day, month, and year out loud as well as the place where you are located. All this helps to ground you in the here and now.

The Keyboard

Sit in a chair with your eyes closed and imagine you're going to the corner of the room to look at yourself objectively. Feel a strong sense of neutrality toward yourself, as if you were looking at another person. Imagine that in that corner is a piano-type keyboard on which each key expresses a distinct feeling or mood. Create a mood simply by pressing a particular key. Some good ones to try are exhilaration, grief, anger, confusion, self-pity, anxiousness, and amusement.

As you press the key, go back to the center of your head and imagine as fully as possible that you are "in" that mood. Feel it totally and completely. *Be* it.

The point of this exercise is to create the mood, fully believe in it for several moments, and come out of it quickly. After the exercise is over, focus your attention in the center of your head, say your name to yourself, and feel your grounding.

Chapter Four

Visualization and Transformation

The human psyche of every individual is made up of mental pictures that tell us who and what we are. Most of us believe we *are* those pictures, which makes it difficult to impossible to create major changes in our lives. How do these pictures work in our everyday life?

All day we're busily absorbing life's experiences. Part of us is like a nonstop camera, filming reels and reels of experiences. Technically, these reels are composites of thousands of single frames, or pictures. For practical purposes, we will define the term *picture* as a portion of a movie reel containing a specific theme.

When we are in harmony with or neutral to the events surrounding us, the pictures we absorb will be neatly filed in our memory banks. But when we have a traumatic reaction to an event, the picture can't be stored away so easily. It keeps on moving through our aura and, whether we know it or not, keeps us very busy and consumes lots of energy.

How? Such "charged" pictures continually send out their own distress signals and are constantly attracting experiences just like the one that created the charged picture in the first place! The bigger the picture's emotional charge (your reaction), the stronger the forces that attract like events into your aura and your life.

By practicing the visualization exercises presented in this book, it should become obvious that your inner eye can literally focus on any picture you choose. The ability to focus is determined, naturally, by your individual interest and aptitude. In all cases, this picture-making process is invaluable, for it is the tool of change within us. Its importance has been vastly belittled, misunderstood, and underestimated in our modern world. Yet in reality, it is the secret link between our thoughts and what happens to us in our daily lives. That which continually presents itself to us in life "from the outside" is not as arbitrary as most people believe. The relationship between the mental pictures each of us carries and what actually becomes our reality is undeniably a cause-and-effect relationship. Every thought-form that dwells inside us and projects itself outward has a constant effect on what we experience in the world.

Our physical form is surrounded by an energy field that can be seen and measured by Kirlian photography and other scientific methods. In metaphysical terms, this energy field is called the "etheric body." It mirrors the condition of the physical body and forms an important aspect of the aura that surrounds and permeates each and every one of us. The aura has been defined in many ways, but it's sufficient for our purposes to think of it as an envelope of energy that projects our thoughts and feelings, both consciously and unconsciously.

The etheric body is constantly absorbing vital energies from the earth, sun, and the cosmos. At the same time, it serves as a matrix for holding thought-forms, or mental pictures. Our personality uses these thought-forms to define who and what it is. The etheric body is the link between mental projections and actual experiences in the physical world.

Scientists have seen that all physical matter is simply energy vibrating at various frequencies. Your physical body is like a radio signal to the outside world, vibrating at frequencies that broadcast exactly who you are. Your vibration constantly affects your cellular development and your nervous system. The rate of vibration—your own particular radio signal—is constantly influenced by the mental pictures you maintain!

To understand the relationship between a mental picture and your physical vibration, think of the effect certain ideas or moods have on your vitality. Compare how energetic you feel when you get up early to leave for a vacation versus arising early for work. How does your body feel when you're sad or angry compared to when you're in love?

Experience also shows that the signals you send out will attract similar signals in return. Again, compare this with a radio transmitter and receiver: If you send a message out to the world in one language, you're most likely to get replies in that same language. This phenomenon is reflected in the karmic law that says the universe gives you a perfect reflection of what you present to the world—or, as the Bible says, "You reap what you sow." This concept is not necessarily a moral issue, but rather a *scientific mechanism*: your everyday thoughts extend into the future like a blueprint, making you the architect of your own life.

True understanding of this concept helps answer such common questions as: "Why do I keep having the same things happen to me? Why do I keep repeating the same mistakes?" In a nutshell, the answer is that you haven't neutralized those charged pictures that have become a powerful inner blueprint. If you want to grow out of certain problems and patterns, you have to learn to "discharge" the pictures that hold the unwanted patterns in place.

Fortunately, there are many ways of discharging pictures. The amount of work it takes depends on the tenacity of the pictures. Going into therapy can release charged pictures, and so can talking to a friend and having a good cry. You can also discharge pictures on a subconscious level in your dreams. Or you can do it through meditation and guided visualization, as explained in the next two exercises.

Changing a Picture

Think of a very happy or pleasant picture you are keeping, and then find a very unpleasant one. Put them side by side on the movie screen of your mind. Imagine that all the energy from the pleasant picture will flow over to the unpleasant one and neutralize its effect so that it no longer feels unpleasant.

Try experimenting the next time you feel emotionally upset. If you're experiencing mental pain, look at that pain simply as a picture. Go to the center of your head and pick out a happy picture from your collection. Put that picture right next to the painful one and imagine that the delight and joy of it will flow into the pain and transform its energy into that of contentment.

Exploding Pictures

It's important to see how we are all programmed by our experiences in life, and how it is possible to "reprogram" ourselves. One reprogramming method is the "picture changing" explained above, but a more complete and permanent method is "exploding pictures." A picture doesn't have to be a vivid mental image; it can also be a feeling or even a vague sensation. The idea behind exploding pictures is that since the subconscious mind speaks in a language of symbols, it is not only possible to affect a symbol's emotional charge, it's also possible to *replace it* with a more positive and useful one.

Remember, we are all learning valuable lessons from our mental pictures. As we project our pictures out onto the world, they create our life's joys, successes, failures, and problems—they become our experience. The chance to solve our problems is invaluable. We needn't run away from our problems or try to outwit them, because wading through the mire of life is a vital part of learning.

Neutralizing pictures may or may not help you to solve a problem immediately. If you need more experience and learning from a specific problem, you'll surely come in contact with other charged pictures to help you receive your valuable lessons. It's often necessary to neutralize a multitude of similar pictures to reach the "key', picture behind it all. Exploding a key picture may not happen very often, but when it does, you'll most likely feel marvelously light and free.

To explode a picture, create a beautiful rose in front of you. Inside the rose, place the mental picture you would like to neutralize. Just imagine you're "cleaning house" for the day and you're finding and neutralizing anything that gives you a sense of uneasiness or pain.

Find a picture or a feeling concerning any negative or uncomfortable situation you can think of. Out of your vast photo album, consider pictures of guilt, shame, irritation, inadequacy, anger, fear, and so on. Say hello to these pictures! Place one picture at a time inside the rose and allow the whole thing to explode. If you prefer, allow the rose to become very small and explode, or just let it disappear in any way it wants to. No matter what method you choose, the process should be quick and deliberate. Be sure to make the rose release a flash of light to symbolize your life-force energy being set free.

This process doesn't mean you'll simply "forget it all" and not have to act on your problems. More likely you'll be able to deal with your problems more effectively because you are becoming much more objective. Remember, you may or may not be able to solve a problem immediately! If you genuinely need more experience and learning via a particular picture/problem, you'll surely connect with the right ones at the right time.

You'll also need to feel your own sun essence after exploding your pictures, because you need to adjust to the higher energy that the neutralizing of pictures provides. Imagine this life-force energy returning to a sun above your head. Visualize a large, warm, golden sun shining brilliantly there. Say hello to it. Imagine all the released energy that has been locked up within those charged pictures returning to this golden sun in a flash of light.

Using the symbol of the sun invites your highest creative essence, or higher self, to enter your etheric body. Bring this imaginary sunlight into your entire body, all the way down to your toes. Imagine this golden light filling any spaces that were occupied by the pictures floating around in your aura. Feel it filling you entirely, then radiating outward about three feet around you. Be in the center of your head and say the date (day, month, and year). Feel yourself to be one hundred percent focused in present time.

Chapter Five

Going with the Flow

To transform your life, all the levels of your being must be willing to "go with the flow." That is, you must be willing to let go of old, limiting patterns, trust the universe, and surrender to your destiny. This doesn't mean your life is without direction; rather, it means that, like a sailboat, you use the powers of nature to steer your life's vessel in the direction that's right for you. The prospect of going with the flow can bring up fear and resistance, but ultimately it is the most rewarding and time-efficient attitude to maintain. The following exercises will help you determine to what extent you are really willing and eager to step beyond old patterns and pictures and create new, perhaps unknown, possibilities in your life.

Running Energy

"Running energy" is an excellent way to get rid of tension and worry, stay neutral, avoid illness, and feel the strength and vitality of your physical and psychic systems working together. Running energy is about freely receiving and letting go. Stated another way, it is a means of moving along naturally with the flow of life. Stop rowing and start sailing!

After grounding yourself, imagine you're absorbing energy from the cosmos through the top of your head. Allow this energy to flow gently downward along the back of your spinal column, all the way to the base of your spine. Be gentle with yourself. Too much energy brought in too fast can cause imbalance. Visualize the earth energy coming up through your legs mixing with the cosmic energy flowing down through the top of your head.

Metaphorically speaking, the base of your spine is the meeting place of heaven and earth. You can consciously see these two important forces meeting and blending. Make sure you allow for a good balance between the two. For example, if you're feeling dizzy or "not all here," bring more earth energy into your system. If you feel too heavy and earthbound and want to "let go" more, bring a higher proportion of cosmic energy in through the top of your head.

All these adjustments need to be made on a creative, feeling level rather than with your rational mind. This may challenge your beliefs about what you can "know" and what you can do. Tell your intuitive side how happy you are to be giving it more of a say in your life. Tell it what a great thing it is to learn new things.

Once you sense the difference between earth and cosmic energy flowing through your body and have experienced balancing and harmonizing the two, you can try the following exercise. Visualize an old-fashioned pair of scales. On each side is an equal weight: one side says "earth" and the other side says "cosmic." After running energy for a while, take a look at your earth/cosmic scales. Are the scales in balance? You may discover you need a lot more cosmic energy than you thought, or the other way around. You can balance your scales by imagining you're opening up your crown for more cosmic energy, or opening up your feet for more earth energy.

After you have established the proper balance of earth and cosmic energies—and this will vary from day to day—feel the energies blending and harmonizing in the area of your pelvic cradle at the base of your spine. Then imagine these blended energies flowing gently upward along the front of your spine. Allow them to connect all the major energy centers along your spinal column into one comfortable flow.

Finally, release this energy through your crown. It's helpful to imagine the downward-flowing cosmic energy being more toward the back and the upward-flowing blended energies being more toward the front. While releasing energies through your crown, you can feel them rather close to your forehead.

The most difficult aspect of this exercise is usually doing everything simultaneously. If so, practice the parts separately until you feel familiar with each sensation. Begin with grounding, then practice running cosmic energy down along the spine, then run it upward and out the top of your head. Finally, try both parts together. Strive to experience the energy rather than just the intellectual concept.

Feeling these exercises in your body is the key to making them real. This may come as a feeling of general relaxation, sensations of warmth or tingling, deeper breathing, color impressions, energizing joy, or any number of other sensations your body might perceive.

And remember this takes no effort! One good way of avoiding effort is to imagine you are open to whatever the earth and the cosmos have to offer in every moment. Then allow those energies to simply run through you.

If you are prone to headaches or a buildup of pressure in your head, you may need to release more energy out the top of your head. Check to see how much tension you create by "holding on." Sitting in a chair with your head and arms dropping down between your knees, imagine any excess energy in your head flowing out and being absorbed by the earth. Do this in a gentle and consistent manner.

Some people with high energy levels tend to run too much energy at too high an intensity. This can be harmful to your body and uncomfortable for those around you.

Consider whether your aura is extending too far outward. If you feel this is happening, imagine a knob or valve representing your ability to turn the intensity down to a more comfortable level. If this sounds simplistic, remember that such visualizations can have an immediate effect because of the powerful way your subconscious mind works with symbols.

Run energy as much as you like throughout the day. To begin with, I recommend practicing for at least five minutes several times a day. Keep increasing the amount of time, getting used to running energy while you work, rest, and so on. You don't have to be inactive or meditating to do it, either. Once you become familiar with the physical feeling, you can run energy anytime and anywhere. Just say to yourself, "I am now running energy," and find the feeling in your body. At a certain point, you'll be able to do it without thinking about it.

Earth/Cosmic Color Breathing

A creative variation of running energy is "color breathing." Below are four earth/cosmic energy breathing visualization exercises that will help you cleanse and revitalize your aura. Try listening to some quiet music while doing them. Sit comfortably in a chair, feet flat on the floor. Be in the center of your head, ground yourself, clean out your psychic territory, and bring in your sun. Don't force your breath. If you begin to feel lightheaded from too much deep breathing, run your energy for a while without the extra breathing part. Notice how color breathing enhances the power of running your energy.

Color Breathing Exercise No. 1:

Inhale orange earth energy through the energy centers in

your feet, feeling it rise up your legs to your pelvic cradle. Then exhale this energy down your grounding cord, letting go of any old qualities or resistance you might have to the color orange. If you have trouble visualizing the color, imagine your feet sitting in a bucket of liquid orange. If it still doesn't work, imagine healing energy moving upward and downward with each inbreath and outbreath. Do this for several minutes. Experiment with other colors and feel the differences among them.

Color Breathing Exercise No. 2:

Inhale light blue cosmic energy through your crown and let it flow down along the back side of your spine into your pelvic cradle. Then exhale this cosmic energy upward from your pelvic cradle along the front side of your spine and gently out the front of your crown. Let go of any old qualities or resistance you might have for the color light blue. Continue to circulate this light blue energy with each deep inhalation and exhalation, but don't force your breath. If you have difficulty visualizing this color, imagine you're breathing in the blue sky through your crown. Imagine light blue moving up and down with each inhale and exhale. Check your grounding cord and stay well grounded. Do this exercise for several minutes. Experiment with other colors and feel the differences among them.

Color Breathing Exercise No. 3:

As you inhale, bring a wave of yellow earth energy up the front part of your body, beginning with your feet and moving up to the top of your head. Rest your hands on your legs and feel the energy in your hands and arms. As you exhale, see the yellow earth energy moving down the back of your body, underneath your legs, and out your feet again. Let go of any old qualities or any resistance you might have to the color yellow. If necessary, visualize your feet in a pan of yellow liquid; or simply visualize a wave of color moving up and down with each inhalation and exhalation. As you observe the color circulating through your body, feel it removing tension and blockage. Allow the color to soothe and massage every part of your inner and outer body. Do this exercise for a few minutes and experiment with different colors.

Color Breathing Exercise No. 4:

As you inhale, bring a wave of light violet energy in through your crown, moving all the way down the back side of your body, underneath your legs to the soles of your feet. As you exhale, see that same light violet energy streaming up the front part of your body, hands and arms included, and going out through the top of your head. Release any old qualities or resistance you might be holding, and be alert to tension and blockage. Do this exercise for a few minutes and experiment with different colors.

Are You Ready for Change?

Sit comfortably with your feet flat on the floor. Be in the center of your head. Now visualize in front of you the word "CHANGE." See how it is written. What style of lettering is the word made of? What color is it? What qualities does it suggest to you?

This visualization should give you some pictures or feelings about your basic reactions to change. Are you afraid of change? Do you welcome it? Is there something or somebody standing in the way of change? If there is a person standing in the way, say hello and have a conversation with that person.

Remember that resisting change is like saying "no" to life and to yourself. We are endlessly changing, transforming, and growing into new, improved versions of our total being. Accept yourself just the way you are right now. Tell yourself that you can change when the need is there. Begin to get in touch with your inner clock, which allows for change when it's necessary. Don't waste energy resisting change, because it happens anyway when the time and place are right. Trust your inner clock to watch its movement and listen to its impulses.

Take another look at your word "CHANGE," and if necessary, clean it off with an imaginary garden hose or a warm shower. Make it bright and clean. Fill this word up with your sun essence. Say hello to it and notice what it looks like now. Do you feel better about the concept now, or will it take some work? If you want, bring this beautiful word into your heart center. Come out of the exercise by bending over and feeling any tension in your body slipping easily into the ground.

Perfect Pictures and Complaining

"Perfect pictures" are those about perfection, about "how things should be." "If it were like this, then I would be such-and-so," or "If I'm not such-and-so, then I'm not OK." A perfect picture represents discontentment and denial of the here and now. It's looking for an event that has to occur before you can allow yourself to be OK or happy. How often do you relate to your life in this way? Remember, happiness only happens in the here and now! Check out the following list of "perfect-picture" thinking:

1. If the sun would only shine, then I might be in a better

mood. (And for a sunny day: If only I hadn't forgotten my sunglasses.)

2. If you really loved me, then you would understand how I feel.

3. If I were a nice enough person, I wouldn't have gotten divorced.

4. If I were really a good parent, I wouldn't have gotten so angry with my child.

5. I first need to change my attitude before I can love myself.

6. If I could only solve this problem with my mother, then I could finally be the person I'm supposed to be.

7. If I were really good at visualizing, it would be as clear as it is with my physical eyes.

8. If I were really intuitive, I would always know what was going on.

9. If only I didn't have so many perfect pictures!

Living with perfect pictures can incite harsh judgment and make it very difficult to go with the flow or forgive yourself and others. One consequence of having too many perfect pictures is the tendency to complain, either silently or out loud. It's easy to complain, but only at the expense of your state of mind! Notice if you are the type of person who finds enjoyment in complaining. Complaining may be a great way of drawing needed attention to ourselves, but unfortunately, the side effects are most unpleasant: it lowers energy and pulls down the energy of those around us; it nurtures old, unhealthy patterns; and it encourages us to dislike ourselves. Complaining also hampers the influx of new experience.

As an exercise, spend a day noticing how often you and the people around you complain. Become aware of what your perfect pictures are. Say hello to them and begin to realize how they might be keeping you from fully experiencing the present moment in all its glory. Try neutralizing some in a rose. And remember, you're fine just the way you are!

Flowing Needs Forgiving

If you still have a hard time "going with the flow," you might need to look at the importance of forgiving. We can't grow unless we let go of old pictures about "what went wrong." We need to experience what a mistake is, understand its implications, and plan to do better next time. Our "what went wrong" pictures can teach us a great deal about ourselves, but if not handled deftly, they can also cause us to stay stuck.

We need to learn to forgive ourselves for our mistakes. If we don't forgive, we stifle our learning, and we keep love at a distance. When we're not able to forgive ourselves, we can't really love ourselves. The same goes for forgiving and loving others. Each time we're able to forgive, we remove dams that prevent the natural flow of life-force energy, revitalizing areas that were once stagnant.

Also, when we blame others for our problems, we abdicate responsibility for our life. By forgiving others, we take more responsibility for our own transformation. By forgiving, we begin to live in the present moment. We become capable of trusting ourselves, of trusting life.

Forgiveness doesn't come easily for some people. Many believe that it takes lots of effort to forgive. Actually, the well of forgiveness is always around to tap into if we are open and willing. Forgiveness is intrinsic to our nature, and the following exercise will help you experience this.

The Pink Forgiveness Cloud

Lie down or sit in a chair. Imagine a big, pink cloud of forgiveness in the room. Out of that cloud comes a line of energy, looking like a pink rope or string, going to your heart center. Allow yourself to feel the energy of endless forgiveness. This energy is available whenever you need it. Stay connected to this cloud for a while, filling your heart and then putting it wherever else your body might need it.

If you need to forgive others, imagine the life-force energy of the pink forgiveness cloud streaming through your heart center and going to the person you want or need to forgive. Remember, forgiveness is limitless!

Chapter Six

Dealing with the Dark Side

No matter how spiritually educated we become, we'll most likely feel in a bad mood occasionally. And no matter how loving our hearts may grow, we'll probably watch ourselves become irritated now and again about insignificant matters. Living consciously doesn't mean we have to become angelic. The dark side of our nature is part of being human, just as the roots of trees need to grow deeper into the dark earth to be able to balance the many branches reaching toward the sky.

What aspects of yourself do you dislike the most? What do you consider negative in yourself? What part of yourself would you rather not deal with? What things are you afraid of? Answering some of these questions may give you the chance to accept and own up to all of your feelings—whether good or bad, in your opinion—and give you the chance to be more yourself. Only when you're able to look from the vantage point of wholeness concerning good, bad, and ugly can you expect to have greater access to clarity and knowledge.

To feel really happy, you need to know what unhappiness is, and the other way around. The more real your unhappiness (meaning the more you've recognized it), the more intense your happiness can be.

Unfortunately, most of us have been conditioned throughout life to disown the negative aspects of ourselves.

While growing up, we've learned how to cleverly hide much of the embarrassment these negative aspects represent. Consequently, our negativity—or what we *believe* is negative—is repressed because we were never taught how to discharge or neutralize it in a healthy way. The big question about negativity is not "Do you have it?" but rather "What are you going to do with it?"

Acknowledging Fear and Negativity

A way to grow more grounded in your life is to recognize and acknowledge your fears. Having fears about yourself and the outside world inhibits your mind and body when circumstances don't warrant it. Fear is one of the oldest human emotions, and it plays a very necessary role in our survival. Yet as individuals we need to ask ourselves, "Which fears are useful, and which ones are not?"

The problem with fear is that it can become unapproachable by its very nature. If we don't acknowledge it, fear rapidly accumulates and changes into resistance. And the more we resist something, the more obsessed we become with it. What we fear actually becomes a part of us. The more we push away what scares us and the longer we avoid facing it, the more power it holds over us.

It can be illuminating to see how many fear pictures you've accumulated over time. Take some time to quiet yourself and identify your fears. How much do these pictures guide and influence your life blueprint? Many of our fear pictures are not even ours. They have been gathered from others. How many fears have you borrowed from your parents, family members, and friends?

If you're busy owning up to your fears and feelings, you might be interested in such therapies as psychosynthesis, bioenergetics, co-counseling, gestalt, Reichian therapy, etc. Because our negativity, resistance, and fears are always stored in our body, it may also be desirable to work on neutralizing them through various intuitive bodywork methods, including Rolfing, rebirthing, bioenergetics, the Feldenkrais method, or the Alexander technique, etc.

But, before you get too worried about your fears, please try the following: allow yourself to neutralize pictures about fear and negativity simply by owning them (saying hello to them) and exploding them in a rose to regain your life-force energy. Notice how much fear and negativity can dwindle to insignificance simply by neutralizing your long-held mental pictures.

Obstructed Abundance

Many people are balancing their lives with so-called abundance meditations. Even more important than increasing the size of your bank account, abundance is vital to your journey through the land of growth and change. Creating abundance is not only creating the ability to receive, it also represents the amount you *allow* yourself to receive. Many of us would say "I'm very good at that," but ask yourself how often you are uncomfortable receiving compliments or gifts. Many of us tend to turn down compliments very subtly, even though we say thank you or act grateful.

Much of the information feeding our abundance machine is hidden deep in our subconscious, where it's difficult to access. Often we do things that sabotage our abundance without even knowing why. Once we become familiar with what it means to love and accept ourselves, it becomes easier to see how our abundance machine either supports or rejects us.

For instance, envision a highly capable woman going to an interview for a really great job—not only a fun job, but well-paying, too. First, she arrives late for the appointment because of various unforeseen delays. Not only does she dress inappropriately, but she proceeds to make lots of pointless comments to the interviewer, coming across as something less than intelligent. Of course this woman totally fails the interview, even though she actually wants the job very much! Why? Because there may be something sitting in her subconscious that can't allow for advancement. Maybe because she thinks she's not attractive enough. Or maybe her father always told her she wasn't very capable and she still believes it. Or, maybe she needs this experience of loss to learn more about herself in relation to others.

More examples of how the abundance machine works can be found in relationships. Many people find it difficult to receive love. It makes no sense, but how many of us have this problem? We can also apply the concept of abundance to spiritual development. To what extent do you allow yourself the unconditional love and care that is always available to you from your spiritual guides and helpers? How often do you think you are alone, when in reality you are being constantly looked after by your unseen friends? How often do you accept new spiritual information?

You might have the mistaken notion that the concept of abundance clashes with spiritual traditions of detachment, selflessness, and modesty. Yet the philosophy of abundance has nothing to do with attachment or greediness. It's merely our ability to receive, to enjoy the richness of our earth's treasures in many different ways. Furthermore, you can't give unless you are able to receive. It's a two-way street.

Tuning Up Your Abundance Machine

Using visualization, there are some great ways to give your abundance machine a tune-up. In the following exercise, you are going to use a powerful symbol to discover more about your own abundance levels.

Be in the center of your head, and in front of you create a meter with a pointer and a scale going from zero to one hundred. Visualize the words "my present-time abundance meter" underneath. This will symbolize your ability to have and receive. Zero means you don't allow yourself anything, and one hundred means you can receive it all.

Ask the pointer on your abundance meter to show you a number between zero and one hundred. Allow it to happen on its own. All you have to do is watch. What number does it point to? This number represents the percentage of all the good things being offered to you that you can actually accept. Say hello to this number and accept it for what it is. Don't judge yourself harshly if it happens to be lower than you think it should be. Remember, you can only change something by first accepting it.

Now, through the following visualization exercises, we will raise whatever number you have on your abundance meter by five percent. Why so little? Because healthy growth and change is usually most lasting when it is steady and gradual, giving you time to integrate it into the rest of your life.

Before you raise your number by five percent on the meter, look at the area where your pointer will be moving. Ask that part of the meter to show up as a color, symbol, or picture to indicate what might be keeping you from raising your abundance level. Is it your mother? A bad experience with a schoolteacher? Is it fear? Or is it just a vague feeling of your own limited self-image?

Say hello to all of this information, then clean it out of the meter by putting it in a rose and exploding it. Put your lost energy back into the sun above your head and fill the meter with your own sunlight, representing your highest creative essence. Raise the hand on the meter five percent or more, if that feels all right. Then celebrate your increased abundance! Feel it in your body as well as your mind.

Not only can you create all-purpose abundance meters, you can create specific meters as well. For instance, you can create abundance meters for relationships, health, material prosperity, or more openness to your intuition and spiritual guidance. You can even create an abundance meter for how you use your time, and allow yourself all the time in the universe to relieve nervousness and stress. Anything you'd like to increase or improve can be aided by the powerful symbol of the abundance meter.

Understanding Illness

Many people assume that physical illness is a sign of wrongdoing. If you are one of these people and happen to be sick, this kind of judgment may make you even more sick and frustrated. It's true that physical illness may signal that our dietary, mental, or emotional attitudes are hurting us, and this should be taken into consideration. However, physical illness may also indicate that the body is merely bringing itself "up to date." Each time the vibration of our spirit is raised through a learning process, the physical body must follow suit and make accommodations for the important inner changes. When you experience an intense period of growth, you may come down with a cold or some other minor illness. The body is simply registering that it feels unsafe because of the changes and would prefer to hold onto the old, familiar patterns, however troublesome they may be.

For those who can't bear to face up to certain problems and tasks, illness can also be a subconscious excuse not to carry through. Like complaining, being ill can be a way of attracting attention. Illness can also be a time of purification and rest, a time to listen to yourself and to make necessary adjustments in your life. You need to know when to push yourself further and when not to. To do this, you need to develop a good level of self-awareness, which you can gain from lying in bed contemplating your sick body.

When you're ill, it can help tremendously to know the deeper meaning. The following exercise is an easy yet powerful means of getting the desired information you need.

Sit or lie comfortably and ask the illness or pain to appear to you in the form of an animal. Welcome the animal and say hello to it. Keep doing this in your mind until the animal notices you and reciprocates. Converse with the animal, and ask why it manifests itself as pain, illness, or any other physical discomfort. Ask the animal what it needs to transform itself into health. Does it need something imaginary or something physical? Does it need you to do something—or *not* do something anymore? What is the basis of this illness—emotional, physical, mental, or spiritual level?

Ask yourself whether you can—or even want to!—fulfill these needs in the near future. Thank the animal and let it wander away contentedly to its natural surroundings. Wave goodbye to your animal friend. Now visualize that you are filling your body with your own sun energy, especially the parts that held pain or illness. Feel the new warmth, light, and the comfort. Care for your body and love it as you would your own child.

Sometimes regaining your health can be a long process, and in these cases you might want to use the above visualization on an ongoing basis. Maybe a different animal will show up each time you do it, or maybe the same animal will come up with different messages and conversations. This is fine, because you may be coming in contact with different levels of the illness' underlying patterns. Not everything has to be done inside your mind! Remember that the animal can also give you very practical advice about the physical aspects of treatment, including your need to see a doctor, naturopath, or spiritual healer.

Chapter Seven

Psychic Boundaries

The energy field that surrounds us—the human aura—projects all that we are to the outside world, while assimilating information from the outside. Because the human aura functions as a repository for random energies, it's important to recognize our individual degree of vulnerability and our potential to make conscious choices about what we're accumulating.

It's amazing how much information, useful and otherwise, a person can absorb in a single day. To take more control of the input level means developing a consciousness capable of making choices and taking responsibility for what has been absorbed. To take this responsibility for ourselves and our reality is to consciously own the "psychic space" surrounding and permeating us, to make it belong completely to ourselves. This seems so logical, yet few of us actually take charge of our psychic boundaries.

Probably the biggest barrier to taking charge of our psychic "space" is the fact that human beings, consciously or subconsciously, tend to want to control each another. Also, the right to know ourselves and to stand up for what we are often generates tension and guilt for ourselves and those around us. Another reason it's easy to forget about psychic boundaries is that most everyone feels inadequate at times, and some people expect *others* to be responsible for the condition of their psychic space and state of mind.

The best way to understand psychic boundaries is through experience. Imagine you are surrounded and permeated by an energy field called your aura, and that you can feel it extending out from your body about three to four feet. Where your aura ends and the rest of the world begins could be called your "psychic boundary."

The size and intensity of your aura can vary tremendously depending on your mood, character, health, and so on. It's important to know that if your aura is radiating outward more than usual—perhaps even filling up an entire room—it is more exposed to whatever influences are present. For this reason, you need to become aware of how far your aura extends. If you are an intense or outgoing person, it might be a good idea to pull your boundaries closer around you. In this way, you become more concentrated and focused, and you don't run the risk of invading other people's psychic territory. Pulling your aura in to about three to four feet should work well, and you should find yourself much less vulnerable—and less provoking—this way.

You can also become aware of the energies that regularly invade your psychic space. By intuitively making conscious separations between your own energy and ideas and those of other people, you begin learning how to differentiate, knowing what is coming from yourself and what is not. This learning process can be difficult, because the aura is being constantly bombarded and filled with outside information. More often than not, we believe the confusion originates from within. But this is not always true. To get clear on this subject, try the following exercise.

Cleaning Out Your Aura

Whenever your mind and being are confused or cluttered, you can literally "clean up" your aura by using some powerful visualization tools. While cleaning your aura, you will consciously know what is "yours" and "not yours." Sit down in a chair, with your feet flat on the floor and your hands apart. Imagine a whirlwind movement beginning at the floor that moves upward and encircles you. This whirlwind will gently collect the pictures, thoughts, moods, ideas, and desires of all the people with whom you've been in contact—in person and even psychically through projected thoughts.

As the whirlwind spins upward, feel that you're putting all these other people and their energies "out of your space." See this extraneous energy spinning off the top of your head and being deposited anywhere outside your psychic boundary. Know that it is being released and neutralized, and that you don't have to be responsible for it anymore.

Make these separations from others without guilt. Sense why it's OK—even important—to take the time and care to focus completely on yourself. If you find it difficult or impossible to focus on yourself, imagine that you are the only one in the universe. Make sure that family and close friends are also "out of your space." If this presents a problem, imagine you have left all your thoughts and cares about these special people outside the door and can connect with them again after you're finished. Remember, this is like a healing walk in nature: you need to do it alone.

There are several other effective ways to clear the territory within your psychic boundary. One of these is to imagine that a warm shower is raining above you, washing your entire aura clean of clutter. Another excellent method of aura cleaning is to imagine everything you don't want being flushed down your grounding cord and into the earth. Or, use the image of fire burning away old junk.

After your psychic territory has been cleaned, come into the present moment by filling up the spaces that were occupied by other people's energy. Do this by visualizing a large, golden sun shining directly above your head. This highest creative essence of yours is available anytime you need it. Imagine this sun energy moving into your body, all the way down to your toes, and extending outward to completely fill your aura. Feel this sun energy reclaiming 100 percent of the psychic territory that had been taken over by others. To get a distinct feeling of where your boundary is, imagine that the sunlight, together with your aura, extends about three to four feet outward, protecting you without the slightest effort.

Say your name to yourself inside the center of your head and feel your own unique vibration. Say the date to yourself and feel yourself to be totally focused in the present moment. Focus on your heart area and say your name to yourself again. Imagine that any part of your being you might have left anywhere else will now be returned to your solar plexus area—as if your solar plexus were a large magnet attracting its own energy back to itself. Imagine you are recharging your own batteries, so to speak.

Notice how you are breathing during this exercise. Imagine that each breath is filling you with your own sun essence and is moving all the way down into your belly and pelvis area.

The Rose Neutralizer

The rose symbol can be used effectively as a psychic buffer between yourself and others. Using roses as neutralizers is especially good for people who easily become dizzy, confused, agitated, annoyed, or fearful in the presence of other people. If you tend to feel overwhelmed by the intensity of others, you need to be able to comprehend the size of your aura and consider using a rose as protection.

Imagine there is a rose, or several roses, between yourself and the other person or people. The roses will absorb and neutralize any unwanted energy corning toward you. You can create hundreds of roses on the outside edge of your entire aura for protection. Grounding yourself, running energy, feeling your sun, and taking deep breaths can be of great help as well.

Neutrality

Did you know that the more we resist something, the more we're likely to be stuck with it? When we resist something, we project psychic energy to keep it away, but as this "something" moves toward us, it gets caught in our aura. Two opposing forces or energies come to a deadlock within our psychic territory and can't move. In this way, we literally attract what we resist!

Consider the common phenomenon of children resisting the idiosyncrasies of their parents, only to grow up acting just like them. Or, when is the last time you resisted someone else's boredom or problems and ended up being bored or in a bad mood yourself?

Resistance is related to our desire to control the "random input level" of the energies entering our aura. The problem with resistance is that it doesn't work the way we want it to! What does work is neutrality or nonresistance. Neutrality is a practical means of choosing one's amount of involvement, with an eye out for the highest good.

In spite of any programming we might have had about the necessity to sympathize with others, it may not always be desirable or appropriate. If we become too sympathetic and emotionally involved, we lose our valuable composure, which may only add to the other's problems.

Don't try to take someone's problems away. Problems are created by our higher self to learn and grow. It's important that each of us be given the chance, to some degree or another, to solve our own problems. We can certainly assist each other and lend our heartfelt support. But if we take a problem away from someone entirely, there's a good chance they'll create that problem in some other form, later. Some people may even become resentful or get angry at you for taking away their problem!

Going into sympathy with someone can cause us to lose our more expansive view and our ability to help. It can also create unnecessary distraction and loss of energy. Yet being neutral is not always the solution, either. Sometimes we need to get involved, head over heels, because our higher self has similar learning in store for us. In this case, we need the experience of nonneutrality and all of the distraction and loss of energy it entails. The whole point of neutrality is to know the possibilities within the greater whole. It means stepping far enough back at the onset to make a conscious choice.

Experiencing neutrality can be initiated by imagining you are invisible or like a "body of glass." Imagine that this invisible form or glass body will not resist anything, and that any energy or vibrations (ideas, emotions, and so on) coming from another person will pass right through it without having any effect on you or your aura.

You can even go further and imagine that the foreign energy moving toward you will go in a circle, directly back to the person it came from—like a boomerang. Or visualize that the other person's energy is passing through you and will take care of itself. If you remain neutral, you will maintain your own inner balance and calm. Besides allowing the other person to deal with his or her own problems more effectively, you're also much less likely to be manipulated or controlled.

Remember, being neutral doesn't mean you should be cold and unfeeling. The intent is compassion and respect for each individual's process, including your own. Neutrality is an attitude that enables you to keep in touch with your own information.

Take a look at your relationships with friends and

family to see how often manipulation or control occurs. How often do you want other people to solve your problems for you? How often are you inclined to do it for someone else? If you find an invisible body or a body of glass difficult to imagine, try being in the center of your head and feeling your sun essence totally filling and surrounding you. Get in touch with your grounding cord. Imagine you're at the seashore, where large waves are washing through you. Don't resist the waves. Pretend that darkness can shine through you as well as light, without changing your mood. Visualize an important person walking up to you and through you while you remain unchanged and completely neutral. This last exercise is especially effective with those who invade your psychic boundaries. Practice it several times a day and see what happens.

Grounding and Owning the Room

Another effective way of keeping your space while serving the highest good is by grounding and "owning" the room. Begin by visualizing a thick grounding cord in the center of the room—a cord that is hollow and filled with golden energy. Let any heaviness or negative energy in the room flow down this grounding cord and into the earth, where it will become neutralized. Just imagine this happening, then notice how different the room feels afterward. The room is now ready to receive whatever is for the highest good.

Now ground yourself, making your own cord any color and size you like. Notice the difference between grounding yourself and grounding the entire room.

Next, invite new and pleasant energies into the room. Do this by imagining you are painting the walls, ceiling, and floor a special color. Don't think too much! Just take the first color that comes to mind and feels right. When you are finished painting, notice what it's like to be in this room.

Notice the different atmospheres you are able to create by visualizing different colors on the walls, floor, and ceiling. Try pink, purple, blue, green, yellow, or any other color that comes to mind.

To "own a room" means to feel comfortable in it. To accomplish this, visualize effortlessly pulling all the corners of the room toward yourself as the room stays the same size. Like shaking someone's hand, this is a way of introducing yourself to the room. The room, clearly, is now yours to enjoy; it no longer belongs to the moods or influences that occupied it before.

If you are the kind of person who easily senses the presence of unwanted, intangible beings in a room, simply ask them to leave! Neutralize any fear pictures you might be keeping concerning these beings. Then proceed with the above exercises, and remember to keep well-grounded. Bring your sun intensely into your psychic territory and feel the vibration of your own name. If you follow this procedure, an unwanted entity won't have a fighting chance; not being able to handle your energy level, it will have to look for another lodging.

Chapter Eight

The Practicality of the Chakra System

You have been introduced to the concept of the etheric body and its connection with the physical body. You have also read how the etheric body holds thought-forms that define who and what you are and that absorb vital energies from the earth, sun, and cosmos. Within this etheric realm, there are specific centers of energy and information called *chakras*, also known as "life wheels." The word *chakra* comes from the Sanskrit word meaning "wheel," and was used by yogis of old to describe the perpetual activity of these centers. Chakras are centers of energy that emanate from the body. They aren't specific points you can put your finger on; rather, they are vibrating *cores* of information extending from the front to the back of the body.

The major chakras are correlated with special points aligned along the spine and have a direct relationship with specific physical organs, endocrine glands, and nerve cells.

The functioning of our chakras is of utmost importance because of their direct connection between body, mind, and spirit. It is likely that humans of the future will be as familiar with these energy centers as people of today are with their hands and feet. This chapter will help you develop a working relationship with your chakra system as we examine the seven major chakras located along the spine and head, plus the secondary chakras in the hands and feet.

The reason most people don't know about their

chakras is that they never looked for them! Many people *feel* their chakras but don't correlate the feelings with any specifically defined centers of energy. For example, have you ever had an upset stomach during or after an emotional upheaval, or had "butterflies" in your stomach when you were nervous? Have you felt your chest tighten when you were sad, or felt it "bursting" with excitement or feelings of love? Do you roll your eyes upward when trying to remember something? In each case, you were unknowingly in touch with one of your chakras.

The following is a brief introduction to each chakra, explaining where it is located and what kind of energy it embodies. You'll be amazed how your increased awareness of these centers will enable you to understand yourself.

The Base

The first chakra is located at the base of the spine and surrounds the bowels and reproductive organs. This chakra involves your earth connection and is commonly called the "root chakra." Your root chakra serves as a fountain from which a tremendous amount of vital energy can flow, connecting all the major chakras along the spinal column in one dynamic whole. It's filled with information about your survival and the connection you have with the physical world. It reflects your attitude toward your health and physical condition and the environment in which you live and work. The first chakra also represents the manner in which you manifest your worldly ambitions.

A person who has blockages in the first chakra will likely be learning how to feel safe and how to survive in the physical world. Common ailments associated with the first chakra are hemorrhoids, constipation, and dysfunctions of the reproductive system. The glands associated with the first chakra are the gonads in men and the ovaries in women.

The Belly

The second chakra is located about three fingers below the navel. This chakra concerns emotions and sexual feelings. It is closely related to the first chakra in conjunction with reproduction and the condition of the physical body; yet the second chakra is also a communication center that allows you to sense the feelings and emotions of others to varying degrees of intensity. Some people whose second chakras are wide open experience the feelings of others believing they are their own. Too much receptivity here can lead to confusion and emotional chaos.

On the other hand, blockages in the second chakra may reflect repressed or hidden emotions or difficulty in communicating. These blockages represent emotional imbalance and/or a strong dependency on others for emotional support.

Physical ailments associated with the second chakra are bladder problems and all of the possible ailments described for the first chakra. The glands associated with the second chakra are the adrenals.

The Solar Plexus

The third chakra is at the solar plexus and distributes life-force energy throughout the body. This is your power center, whose purpose is to help you "make" and "do." It expresses the will, enthusiasm, and creativity housed in the physical body.

If you are weak in the third chakra, you may feel habitually tired, depleted, or nervous. It may indicate that you are low in certainty and self-esteem, or that you are leaking energy to those around you. The third chakra is also an "ego control center" that some people use to dominate others. It is closely bound with the second chakra and is easily influenced by emotions. It registers anger, fear, hostility, frustration, and boredom, or enthusiasm, creativity, invigoration, etc.

Other functions of the third chakra are out-of-body experiences and memory, taking responsibility for the practical use of energy, self-motivation, and balancing the art of giving and receiving. If your third chakra is in good working order, you will probably feel ease in completing physical tasks.

Blockages in this center may be revealed in ailments such as stomach and intestinal malfunctions, liver, kidney, and gall bladder problems, exhaustion, and nervous disorders. Like the second chakra, the third is closely connected to the adrenal glands as well as the pancreas.

The Heart

The fourth chakra, the heart chakra, is located at the sternum and shows the love and affinity you feel for yourself and the rest of the world. It is the meeting point between the lower three and the upper three chakras—hence, the synthesis of both earthly and cosmic awareness. The heart chakra is powerfully related to self-image and how much you are able to love yourself. It is connected to the solar plexus chakra in relation to achieving abundance, because you can only receive as much as your sense of self-worth allows. This chakra enables you to experience openness, trust, a sense of wealth and abundance, and unconditional love.

When it comes to emotional closeness and communication, the heart chakra functions closely with the second chakra. The difference between the two is that, while the emotional center often feels the need for physical satisfaction and fulfillment, the heart center can be fulfilled through spiritual affinity. It can experience understanding, compassion, forgiveness, tenderness, and goodwill. Through the heart, we can experience a oneness with the planet and our creator, as well as a vital connection to our deepest source of healing.

If your heart chakra is blocked, you may experience blood pressure regulation and/or circulation problems, difficulty in breathing, chest pains, or physical heart ailments. The gland associated with the heart chakra is the thymus.

The Throat

The fifth chakra is located at the throat and is a powerful center of communication and self-expression. The throat chakra is connected with the physical voice and deals with our ability to express sentiments coming from the heart, belly, and higher perceptions. Its telepathic nature enables us to have mental, nonverbal communication with living things and to hear sounds coming from nonphysical dimensions. The fifth chakra can also speak to us through our "inner voice," a primary intuitive source.

Telepathic messages received at the throat chakra tend to be very practical. For instance, we may know what someone is thinking, when we're going to receive a letter, and so on.

People with fifth-chakra blockages or problems may experience thyroid imbalance, a sore or congested throat, coughs, bronchial or lung problems, loss of voice, or stuttering. Hearing loss may occur if a person cannot deal effectively with certain kinds of fifth-chakra stimulation. The gland associated with the fifth chakra is the thyroid.

The Brow

Your sixth chakra is located at your forehead, between the eyebrows and extending inward to the center of your head. It's commonly called the "third eye." This is your center of visualization and clairvoyance. Your third eye allows you to see energy and to perceive and project reality.

The sixth chakra provides the potential for you to gather information on very expansive levels and to look outside the confines of time and space. It can connect with information that goes beyond the individual personality and into realms of the collective consciousness.

If your ability to focus and concentrate is well developed, this chakra gives you access to a perspective that can transcend emotion and bring you neutrality and objectivity. The sixth chakra enables you to focus on many abstract concepts and insights, and to bring inspiration and innovation into the world. Artists and writers commonly use their brow chakra in combination with impressions coming from lower chakras. For everyone, the sixth chakra holds the potential for growth and change and needs to be viewed in its working relationship with all the other chakras.

If you are out of balance at the brow chakra, you may have eye problems, pressure or pain around the forehead region, or a fever. These symptoms may appear if you are blocked or too wide open and subsequently overloaded with mental pictures and information. In the latter case, dizziness might occur with a sensation of being "not all here." The glands associated with the sixth chakra are the pineal and pituitary.

The Crown

The seventh chakra, located at the top of your head, is commonly referred to as the "crown chakra." Known in Eastern religions as the "thousand-petaled lotus," this is the chakra associated with spiritual wisdom. It represents the culmination and flowering of all your knowledge as a soul.

Information received through this chakra is complex and fertile with subconscious manifestations of your total being. Like the sixth chakra, the highest potentials of the seventh chakra enable you to look outside the confines of time and space, to transcend emotion and personality, and to connect with universal consciousness.

The seventh chakra is the spirit's conscious connection with the physical body. On the most basic level, the seventh chakra enables you to "be still and know." It relates to the entire foundation of human intelligence and experience. Consciously experiencing this level of perception may only last a fleeting moment, yet it's certain that a steadily increasing number of people in our world are actively conveying information from this seventh-chakra perspective.

At best, the seventh chakra is concerned with the welfare of all life and represents an understanding of the creative forces that guide our activities in everyday life. At worst, the seventh chakra can be used to control and manipulate others. Throughout history, charismatic individuals have enjoyed using their seventh-chakra power to either inspire and help or to exploit and dominate others.

Children often become seriously blocked on the seventh chakra level from the influence of overzealous authority figures, including well-meaning teachers and parents. Often, this results in varying degrees of uncertainty, lack of confidence, confusion, and alienation from one's self.

If you are trying to hold on to your energy, or if you have blocks in your seventh chakra, you may experience frequent headaches, a feeling of pressure from inside, or a sensation of having a heavy weight resting on top of your head. Running energy is highly recommended for these ailments to bring a good flow of life force out of the crown. The glands associated with the seventh chakra are the same as those for the sixth: the pineal and pituitary.

Hands and Feet

The palms of your hands and the soles of your feet are equipped with smaller chakras. The chakras on the hands can be used for sending or receiving energy and information. You can run energy in your hands and arms just as you've done with your feet and legs. Imagine you have a flower in the palm of each hand that will open up when asked. Or pretend your hand chakras are like camera lenses, opening and closing with ease.

Starting from each hand chakra, visualize a golden cord of energy moving up your arms, through your shoulders, and into your heart center. These energy channels from your hands to your heart are called "creative hookups." Connecting your heart to your hands greatly enhances creativity. The energy you run through your creative hookups can be either cosmic or earthly. When you rest your hands with palms upward, they receive more cosmic energy. When you rest them downward, they run more earth energy.

To sensitize your hand chakras, feel the energy field that builds up when you hold your hands facing each other. Try different distances and get the sensation that you are holding different sizes of light bubbles in your hands. You can also feel warmth in your hand chakras—or imagine what it would feel like to catch snowflakes in your palms. Hold one palm outward, fingers spread comfortably. Feel the aura of a pet, a plant, a rock, or a crystal. Be open to differences in temperature and density. Give yourself permission to sense information in the form of colors, pictures, or symbols. Close your eyes and imagine what colors you see around your hands. Ask yourself what the colors mean.

The chakras on the soles of your feet are, as you already know, very useful in drawing earth energy up into your legs and up to your root chakra. This process keeps you grounded and makes your body feel safe and real. Imagine opening up your foot chakras just as you did your hand chakras, like a flower or the lens of a camera. Feel a lovely, warm, tingling sensation in your feet and legs.

Getting to Know Your Chakras

Now that you've been introduced to the chakra system, you can begin to form a friendship with these amazing life wheels, getting to know each one as a vital component of your everyday experience. With the following exercise, it's very helpful to adopt a positive attitude, believing that you are capable of sensing what's happening in your chakras. Don't be concerned about how much or how little information you receive; just allow yourself to be receptive to whatever you perceive.

Be in the center of your head, ground yourself, and clean out your psychic space. Bring in your golden sun. Run your energy for a few minutes. Imagine each chakra as a glowing sensation that you can feel physically. Starting with one chakra at a time, imagine a ball of energy with a specific color or colors. Say "hello" to each chakra individually and wait for a response. The manner in which a chakra says hello back to you can provide a lot of information—be open to it!

With each chakra, get a feeling for the intensity with which it's glowing, how big or little it is, how open or closed, and what colors it is. After doing this, you may want to reread the descriptions of the seven chakras and become more familiar with the qualities each one embodies. If you see any pictures or colors, ask what they mean. If a chakra feels blocked, ask for information about why. If you get in touch with any pictures or emotions that are causing blockage, say hello to them, then neutralize them in a rose.

Finally, fill your chakra with the golden sunlight you have just retrieved from the charged pictures.

As you bring each of your chakras up to date by neutralizing charged pictures, imagine you are writing the current date and your name in your chakras. This makes each chakra more your own. You may also want to visualize other healing colors in and around each chakra. Ask your chakra what color it needs to be more balanced. Some good ones to try are light pink (affinity), light blue (soothing), varying shades of green (new growth and harmonizing), and orange (stimulating).

An interesting approach to healing and helping your chakras is amusement. You can ask a funny picture to appear in any particular chakra to help it flow better. For instance, imagine the chakra making faces, telling jokes, or having a laughing fit. Or throw some confetti around the chakra—whatever fits your own sense of humor.

You may like to finish a chakra meditation by imagining a golden circle of light with a pentagram or equal-sided cross inside. This symbol can be placed over each chakra for protection, just as the symbol of a rose can protect your aura.

Chakra Color Meditation

Traditionally, each chakra is associated with a particular color. The seven colors correspond with those of the rainbow, starting with red at the root chakra, moving up to orange at the belly; yellow or gold at the solar plexus; green at the heart; blue at the throat; indigo at the third eye; and violet at the crown.

The colors traditionally attributed to each chakra also define their different frequencies. Just as the color red has the lowest frequency that can be seen by the physical eyes, the first chakra is the major energy center with the lowest frequency. The next color in line is orange, which is associated with the second chakra and the next highest frequency, and so on, up to the vibratory rate of violet at the crown.

Although very useful, this traditional system is not meant to tell us that everybody's second chakra is orange, or that all heart chakras are green. As we learn to perceive them intuitively, chakras express themselves in all colors. Your own manner of reading your chakras depends on the set of symbols you're using at the time and the way you interpret them. Nevertheless, using the traditional color of each chakra, as in the following exercise, can be an interesting way to get started. It's like using a set of keys to access each one.

Sit with your feet flat on the floor and be in the center of your head. Ground yourself and run your energy. Begin with the root chakra and get in touch with the red vibration: feel it inside and out, even in your grounding cord. Feel what the red vibration is like and what it has to offer. Then go to orange and feel it in your second chakra. Again, meditate upon the color vibration. Tune into yellow for the third chakra, green for the fourth, blue for the fifth, indigo for the sixth, and violet for the seventh. As you surround and permeate yourself with each color, remember to stay grounded and be in the center of your head. As you tune into each color, you may notice them invigorating you and bringing you harmony and clarity.

Chakra Balancing

Each chakra is sympathetic to the system as a whole, meaning that the harmony or disharmony of one chakra will have its effect on all the others. No one chakra is more important than another, although many traditional teachings have stated otherwise. You can't have the lotus flower without the stem! Our higher knowledge is meaningless unless we love and acknowledge the human foundations that support it.

In meditation, be aware of where your chakras are the brightest or the liveliest. Are you top-heavy? Bottom-heavy? Do you feel there is a good balance between earth and cosmic energy in your chakra system?

When running energy up and down the spine, make sure all of your chakras are well connected via the back channels. Do you notice any areas that seem to be blocked? If so, be open to any pictures, colors, or symbols depicting blockage. Have a conversation with the blocked area to help you understand why it's there. If necessary, explode and neutralize pictures in a rose, then visualize lots of golden sunlight occupying that spot.

Chakra Breathing

If you would like to heal a chakra, here is a powerful exercise that can help. Choose the chakra you would like to work with and imagine breathing in and out of it. With each inhalation, breathe in the positive qualities associated with that chakra; with each outbreath, release whatever negative qualities might have become lodged there. In this way, you can regularly "tune" and strengthen each chakra, maximizing its ability to create a positive life experience.

These qualities are only examples. You may find others that are more accurate or appropriate for your particular situation. After doing this special breathing for several minutes, spend several more minutes sitting quietly, imagining that a healing color of your choice, along with the positive aspect you just breathed in, will rest happily in that chakra for the remainder of the day.

Chakra Healing Exercise

	Inbreath	Outbreath
First Chakra	feeling safe, being healthy	unsafe and unhealthy considerations
Second Chakra	humor, gaiety, lightness	heaviness, sorrow
Third Chakra	creativity, invigoration, freedom	stagnation, boredom, worry, frustration, feeling trapped
Fourth Chakra	loving yourself	criticizing yourself
Fifth Chakra	self-expression	muteness, obstruction
Sixth Chakra	clarity	confusion
Seventh Chakra	self-confidence	uncertainty, indecision

Chapter Nine

Chakra Awareness in Relationships

To keep you and your psychic space autonomous, notice the levels on which you communicate and deal with other people. You needn't turn everyday communication into an intellectual exercise or lose your spontaneity, but simply cultivate a natural awareness of which chakras you're using in any given situation—and how you are using them.

The term "corded with someone" means that there is a line of communication going from one person's chakra to another. Envision this communication line looking like a white filament connecting you together on the etheric plane. Having this connection while communicating, you could say the two of you are on the same wavelength. Similarly, without a good cord, you'll feel you're certainly not!

With all the possible communication lines waiting to be used, it is important to take responsibility for what you're activating in others and what they are activating in you. You may feel many different reactions inside yourself as a result of being corded with someone. But the important question is, what do you want to do with it? Cords connecting people can function in respectful or nonrespectful ways, depending on the desires and motives of those involved. With a little practice, you can learn to "look behind the scenes" to determine your manner of involvement with others, both on the giving and receiving side.

You can also learn how to clean out chakra cords once

they've been established. But before you do, it's good to get a totally clear idea about what it might mean to cord with someone on one chakra level or another.

Chakra cords can reflect any number of different connections or relationships. On the one hand, they might reflect learning, help, and interest; on the other, influence, control, and manipulation. It depends on the way they're used. Cords can appear on all chakra levels. And they run horizontally, which means they connect with chakras of the same kind and frequency in the other person.

Knowing which levels you are "cording" with another person gives you the chance to make choices about your involvement. The next time you're having a conversation with someone, notice whether you can sense the presence of a throat chakra cord between the two of you. Or, at a party, look through your third eye at all of the second-chakra cords!

Usually, several kinds of cords appear in the course of normal communication. For example, as two people begin to interact, their interaction creates a throat cord. As the conversation progresses, a second-chakra, or heart cord, may appear. If the two people are talking about new ideas, a sixth-chakra cord might develop between them. If a quarrel arises, this might change into a third-chakra cord.

Chakra cords can vary in size, character, and color: The size of a cord usually shows the level of involvement between two people, friendly or otherwise. A thick heart cord, for example, shows a strong affinity between two people, while a thick third-chakra cord may indicate a high degree of competitive interaction.

The character of a particular chakra cord can be perceived through its appearance. The material or texture of a cord also shows the intention with which it was made. Is the cord soft as silk or hard as steel? Is it warm and light or heavy and dark? The color of a cord tells you about the kind of information coming through it. Red might be something creative, exciting, or painful, while blue could indicate a quiet and peaceful connection. A pink first-chakra cord from a parent to a baby might mean, "I love you and I enjoy caring for you." From child to parent, the same cord can mean, "I need you, don't leave me."

First-chakra cording is a fundamental communication line between children and parents. All young children and their parents need to have this cord firmly established, for it provides the child with information about safety and survival. For instance, if the parent is ungrounded or feeling unsafe, the child will sense this and will most likely feel the same thing. First-chakra cords can also be found between caring adults, although this can also indicate a tendency toward overdependence. Sometimes you can see a first-chakra survival cord being created out of fear. On a tacit level, this cord is saying, "Help—save me!"

Second-chakra cording is a connection on the feeling plane. This feeling can range all the way from simply being sociable to the act of making love. It's a very common cord that reflects all the possible degrees of intimacy. Second, chakra cords can be joyful, loving, and lots of fun. They can also be used to manipulate through flattery or seduction.

Third-chakra cording is usually a meeting between two powers of will. They are commonly created in the world of sports, business, politics, and other competitive endeavors involving "team spirit." A person who needs to become motivated by someone else will often cord that person's third chakra, resulting in a siphoning of the life-force energy of the latter's solar plexus. People who are irritated or angry at each other tend to share a third-chakra cord, too.

Fourth-chakra cording is a way of expressing love, affinity, and appreciation. A heart cord shows understanding and compassion and is especially good for giving validation. But, a heart cord can also show jealousy or too much dependency.

Fifth-chakra cording is possibly the most common. It

involves verbal as well as telepathic aspects. Since the throat chakra is a very creative center, you can often see bright and colorful cords existing there among imaginative or artistic people. Members of an orchestra, for instance, will be strongly connected on this level. A less-admirable aspect of fifth, chakra cording is the ability to broadcast negative thoughts, or to be "bad-vibing" other people. This act can be either unconscious or deliberate.

A sixth-chakra cord appears when there is a vivid exchange of ideas and insights. This is a cord you use, for example, when brainstorming with someone else. It can also serve as a bridge to "get into other people's heads"—meaning that curious people can get closer than you'd like them to! A sixth-chakra cord can also be used to manipulate and control others.

A seventh-chakra cord shows a connection on a spiritual level. It can also serve as a means of communication between teacher and pupil, parent and child, guru and disciple. A crown-chakra cord can be used in a possessive or manipulative way by interfering with someone else's autonomy.

Removing Chakra Cords

Whether we know it or not, we are creating chakra cords endlessly, almost all the time. For most people, this happens naturally and unknowingly. Most cords fade away on their own immediately after being activated or soon after the communication is over. Other cords stick around for a long time, depending on the intensity and duration of the involvement.

You can keep chakra cords alive even though you are no longer physically close to the other person. Time and space are of no importance. Often, keeping a particular connection feels good, and that's why we keep it—for example, a heart cord with a special person.

More often than not, however, we need to dissolve or remove old cords we have been unwittingly keeping, even if they seem like positive ones. Staying in the present moment and being open to new experiences and information is essential to our overall clarity and well-being. This isn't possible if we keep ourselves loaded up with old cords that are not appropriate for our present-time circumstances. Daily communication can become unnecessarily complicated for the simple reason that there's too much information coming through our cords that hasn't been processed.

It's probably not difficult for you to imagine how many people have chakra cords that are simply not appropriate anymore. Many problems under the heading of "generation gap" stem from out-of-date cording. An adult who still has a first-chakra cord with her parents might feel limited and unable to make her own decisions. A cord on this level is outdated because the parents are not responsible for their child's survival anymore. If the cord were removed, both parents and child would feel much more free to be themselves in present time. Cording on other levels—for instance, on the heart level—can be both desirable and beneficial since both parents and child still love each other.

Remember that resisting an unwanted cord doesn't work! If you want to change or modify your cords to other people, you first need to accept the fact that you've got them. As mentioned earlier, saying hello to something you don't like is the best way to begin the process of change.

Removing old chakra cords is essential to our psychic housecleaning. Realize that important chakra cords with family and close friends will return automatically when needed. By getting into the same frame of mind as you did with aura-cleaning, you can systematically disconnect, unplug, or dissolve the many cords created in the course of your daily communication. This can be done at the end of the day when you clean out your psychic space and bring in your sun essence.

One effective approach is to imagine all the cords gently fading away (do not jerk them out!) and disappearing. After they have faded, fill the empty spaces with gold energy from your sun. It can be that simple. However, sometimes you need to know more about a particular cord before it can be cleaned out successfully.

To do this, focus your attention in the center of your head and feel your sun and your grounding. Run your energy for a while. Let somebody come into your thoughts with whom you communicate on a regular basis. This can be your partner, a family member, a friend, or a colleague. The first person who pops into your mind is the one to work with.

While thinking of this person, ask yourself on what chakra levels you usually communicate with them. You can see the answer with your mind's eye, sense it, know it, feel it, or think it—whichever way the information wants to come to you. If you get more than one chakra, that's fine, but right now you need to pick just one to work with. Afterward, you can go back and work with the others.

Clearly see or sense this cord. Is it thick or thin? What are its characteristics, and what sort of physical material does it suggest? What are its colors? Look at the flow of energy in the cord. Is it going in both directions, or is it one-way? Ask yourself if the cord is totally clean or whether it needs to be cleaned out with an imaginary garden hose or dust cloth. Look again at the color(s) of the cord and get a feeling for the sort of messages that are going through it. What are you and this other person sharing? What are you learning together?

If you discover you're keeping an out-of-date cord, imagine you are writing the present date on that cord. When you've done that, it will probably change color, size, and consistency because you reminded it of the power of the present moment. If you find yourself frustrated because you've tried this and nothing has changed, reconsider the purpose of the cord. Maybe you still need to communicate something important through this cord, or perhaps it will have some meaningful purpose in the future.

Chapter Ten

The Inner Teacher

There are so many aspects to spiritual guidance and so many kinds of guides that it's easy to become confused. The primary and most easily available guide is the "inner teacher" who is part of your higher self. He or she is a spiritual guide who is intimately connected with your own soul. Also available are personal guides and helpers, beings who are separate from our souls whom we'll discuss in the next chapter.

There are some important requirements for working successfully with guides. The first is a willingness to learn and be helped. A guide will only meet us halfway; it's up to us to be open to an encounter. The second requirement is that we open up our heart chakra to good communication. An open heart chakra, combined with strong feelings of love and affinity for our guides, can literally set the stage for a successful meeting.

The inner teacher may first appear to you as a color or symbol or some abstract form. If you find it difficult to relate to or communicate with the form in which he or she appears to you, you can ask your inner teacher to change form. While an inner teacher does not have a gender or a nationality per se, such distinguishing details may help you communicate with him or her.

You can ask your inner teacher to help you with anything you like. When you have a difficult encounter with someone, you might ask your inner teacher for understanding. "What am I supposed to be learning from this experience?" you might ask. Your inner teacher can be invaluable in helping you use your intuition, both for yourself and for the benefit of others. Help is always available; you only need to learn how to ask for and accept it.

Before you can get anywhere with your inner teacher, it may first be necessary to neutralize certain thoughts or pictures. You might be asking yourself, "How can I bother a guide with such mundane questions?" Or, "How do I know I can trust this information?"

You'll learn to know when you can trust and when you can't by the quality of information you receive in meditation. As your own truth becomes more and more apparent, so will the natural intuitive reactions that accompany this truth. As a rule of thumb, true guidance offers unconditional love, leaves you free to be totally yourself, and stimulates you to learn in your own unique way. If these qualities are not present, it's highly recommended that you reassess your relationship with that guide.

Finding Your Own Prayer

Before meeting your inner teacher, it helps to prepare yourself by getting inspired. Whether you consider yourself religious or not, praying is a powerful means of connecting to the higher spheres. You can create your own prayer by writing down phrases that mean something important to you—perhaps words from songs, poems, stories, or dream memories. A prayer doesn't have to be long or complex; it can be very short and simple. You may prefer a traditional prayer or a modern one. The only thing required is a deep feeling of connection with the prayer and a sense of heartfelt joy when you say it to yourself. Your prayer can be a creative visualization about how you'd like certain things to be. It can be a prayer for protection, a group blessing, a request for help, or a reminder of how you would like to experience daily life.

Your prayer can be something you don't want to share verbally with anyone else, although it can be very empowering to pray with others. In any case, feel your prayer intensely in your heart center and in every cell of your body. Make it totally real. Repeat certain phrases if you wish and experience the remarkable power of words.

Your prayer may change from time to time, or it may stay the same. Make a regular practice of using your private prayer as a means of receiving help and insight. And remember that this help and insight is always available, twenty-four hours a day.

Your Own Sanctuary

Before you meet your inner teacher, it's also important to create a special place inside yourself—a place where you feel totally safe and peaceful, a wonderful refuge where you can heal yourself and live up to your full creative potential. This sanctuary may be a place in nature. It may remind you of a place you have actually been—a meadow, a forest, a mountaintop, the seashore on a desert island. Or your sanctuary might be in your own house, in a church, on a boat, etc. Perhaps you don't know where it is, but it's an inspiring place that makes you feel absolutely wonderful. The only thing required of this special place is that it always makes you feel safe and peaceful and that it belongs only to you.

Sit comfortably and feel your attention focused in the center of your head. Say hello to yourself inside the center of your head. Then feel your feet and your grounding cord going from the base of your spine (at your first chakra) to the center of the earth. Say hello to the center of the earth. Feel your aura surrounding you. Clean and fill it with your sun essence, as taught in Chapter Seven of this workshop.

Let your mind be free to wander. Allow yourself to be led to your sanctuary easily and without effort. Once you have found it, look around and soak in the views. Listen to the sounds, smell the air, and touch the surroundings. Become aware of any special feelings, distant memories, or abstract impressions this place creates. Build some sort of shelter or comfortable place to sit or lie down if you wish. Do anything else that makes your sanctuary more comfortable or homey.

What would you like to do in this special place? Would you like to sing, yell, jump, dance, laugh, or run? You are free to be totally yourself in your sanctuary. This is a very special place of power for you, a place where you can live up to your full creative potential. Are you looking for new ideas? Do you need inspiration for a particular project? Your sanctuary is a perfect place to become inspired.

Is there any ritual you would like to perform here? Perhaps you'd like to surround the whole area with a protective, golden-white light.

You might notice that your sanctuary spontaneously changes by itself, or maybe you'll find yourself in an entirely new and different place. Allow your thoughts to be adventuresome. Stay open to interesting new impressions. Your creative mind offers endless possibilities.

You can go to your sanctuary at any time simply by closing your eyes and allowing the feelings and impressions to become real. If worries and the stress of everyday life become too much, spend time in your sanctuary for instant healing and rejuvenation.

From the center of your head, be aware of yourself sitting in your chair in meditation. Feel your grounding cord and notice your breathing. Bring your entire sanctuary into your heart center. Feel what it's like to be able to house this special place within your physical body and within present time. Beautiful, inspiring, peaceful places do not have to be far away!

Be in your sanctuary in your heart center. Write your name in your heart center and write the current date. Readjust the openness of all your chakras, if needed, while running energy.

Feel yourself surrounded and filled with golden light from your sun. Give yourself a golden grounding cord. Then come out of meditation by bending over.

Meeting Your Inner Teacher

Now that you've prepared your psychic space, you are ready to meet your inner teacher. This guiding aspect of your consciousness can come to you in many different and changing forms, both human and otherwise. Many people perceive their inner teacher to be simply a vague impression, color, or presence. He or she may change forms, depending on what kind of information or help you need. For instance, if you get too serious about life, your inner teacher may appear as a comedian, helping you get in touch with your humorous side. If you need to become more practical and down to earth, your teacher might appear as a farmer, telling you to wait for better weather.

Seekers often get either a male or a female inner teacher based on which aspect of themselves needs to be brought out more strongly at that time. Similarly, your inner teacher's age, character, and manner of dress can symbolize particular aspects that need examining. Don't necessarily expect verbal communication, because often the inner teacher relates through pictures, symbols, impressions, or a strong sense of knowing.

Sometimes your inner teacher will look like someone you know, showing you similar aspects or possibilities in yourself. This is fine, unless you feel uncomfortable about it. You can always ask your inner teacher to appear in some other form that's easier for you to relate to.

In rare cases, the inner teacher appears as frightening, strict, or authoritarian. Usually this means it's time to look at uncomfortable pictures about yourself, especially from a heart-chakra perspective. Are you too strict or severe with yourself? Do you have low self-esteem? Neutralize these negative pictures in a rose before going further with the inner teacher exercise. Remember, your inner teacher is wise, kind, and loving and is available at all times for guidance, friendship, or help.

Start your meditation by running energy from the center of your head. Feel your body to be very well grounded. Go back to your sanctuary and spend time there feeling comfortable and making yourself at home. When you are ready, imagine there is a pathway within your sanctuary leading into the distance. Begin to walk along this pathway, surrounded by your own sun essence. Feel a deep, inner contentment.

Continue along this pathway for a while and begin to see a distant form emanating a clear, bright light. Allow this form to come closer. As the bright figure approaches, feel the inherent joy its presence awakens in you, and continue to walk confidently in its direction.

As the two of you converge, begin to notice details about your guide's appearance. Is it a man or a woman? What does he or she look like? How old is this person? How is this person dressed? If you don't see anything, allow yourself to receive *feeling* impressions about your teacher.

The closer you get to your inner teacher, the more you may see or perceive of his or her face and demeanor. If you feel fear or resistance, say hello to those feelings and bring in some of your humor. Look your inner teacher in the eyes until you can see lots of golden light and feel him or her in your heart. Greet this radiant being and embrace if you like. Ask his or her name. Now lead your inner teacher back along the pathway to your sanctuary.

Enjoy the silence together. Then ask your inner teacher if there is any special information that should be given to you at this time. If necessary, ask specific questions about an important subject. Your questions may be answered in words, but they may also be answered in pictures, symbols, or feelings. If you don't receive immediate answers, you may get them later in the day or even in your dreams. When you are through, thank your inner teacher and show your appreciation. Ask him or her to come back to your sanctuary another time.

After your inner teacher has left, be in the center of your head again and feel your body sitting in the chair. Say hello to your grounding cord and feel earth energy in your feet and legs. Take this experience of meeting your inner teacher and put it into your heart center. Feel what it's like to be able to house this memory and feeling within your physical body and within present time. Allow your inner teacher in your heart center. Imagine writing your name in it and the current date. Run your energy for a few moments and make sure you're well grounded. Finish by bending over.

Chapter Eleven

Personal Guides and Helpers

Next to the inner teacher, the most common guide is the personal guide. Although not necessarily angels, personal guides are sometimes described as guardian angels. They act as companions and advisers and may have been with you since before you were born. As you grew older, more of them may have entered your life. In fact, by the time a person becomes an adult, he or she may have a number of personal guides. It's normal to experience one guide as being the most influential, while others have their own personal areas of interest or expertise.

For example, one personal guide may concern itself with your physical body and health in general, another with your work and professional activities, another with your family relationships, and still another with your spiritual development. As your life continues to change, your personal guides will come and go. If you are confronted with a particularly difficult task, you may have a guide that helps you specifically with this task. Some guides may stay with you for your entire life—and may even help you between lives. A personal guide is often someone you have known in this or other lifetimes and is here to help you as an old friend and trusted companion.

There are certain things we can do to enhance our relationship with guides. For instance, we may attribute to a guide a special accent or way of speaking. Objects, pictures, statuettes, or jewelry may remind us of our contact with a particular guide and can amplify the realness of it all.

It's very common for a human-like guide to appear in the same form as he or she did in the flesh. Yet, similar to meeting with the inner teacher, a guide's appearance can also symbolize certain qualities of character or experience that he or she is eager to teach us about.

Before they can communicate effectively with their guides, many people need to neutralize pictures having to do with their own "earthbound sin" versus the spirits' "unreachable perfection." If you are confronted with these themes, please have a look at your abundance meter for spiritual guidance. Neutralize your "unworthy" pictures and allow more joy into your life!

It's also important to be able to integrate the guidance we receive. We need to keep our own psychic autonomy intact and not feel we're being overwhelmed by the reality of another, even if it's the guidance of a trusted spirit friend. Always be in present time with your experience and stay well grounded. Realize that it's not the goal for a spirit guide to take us out of this world; rather, its job is to help us better manifest ourselves on this earth. Also keep in mind that many guides are particularly interested in learning from us about bodies and what it means to manifest physically. Our relationship with them is usually a reciprocal learning experience.

Whether you consult your inner teacher or a personal guide depends on what feels the most appropriate to you. Each time and situation is different, and you only need to ask yourself what feels the best.

Meeting Your Personal Guide

To meet your personal guide, begin your meditation by focusing your attention in the center of your head. Ground yourself and run energy with a color you love. Systematically close down your lower three chakras somewhat, one at a time, beginning with the first chakra, at the base of the spine. (It helps to visualize your chakras as camera lenses whose apertures can be opened or closed to allow in more or less light.) Then open up your upper four chakras one at a time, as wide as feels comfortable. Focus on the upper four chakras as one intuitive unit, with the sixth chakra as the central focusing point.

Now create a pink rosebud in your heart chakra, and allow it to grow into a beautiful open flower. Although you may not consciously have met this guide yet, allow yourself a feeling of openness and deep love for your personal guide, like a longing to meet up with an old friend.

While sensing your aura, breathe in and out of your heart chakra. Visualize a large, exquisite rainbow leading down to the edge of your aura, coming from any direction you like. Allow this rainbow to become a multicolored staircase.

After getting in touch with your feelings of love and affinity, allow yourself to perceive a personal guide coming down the rainbow staircase. You may actually see this person, although an abstract impression of color, or a presence, will work just as well. Embrace your guide. Ask him or her for a name. If you need to, ask your guide to change form or appearance for a better connection.

Allow your personal guide to talk with you, sit with you, or even take you on a brief journey. Do whatever you like together. After you have communicated in this way for a while, come back to the center of your head and feel your grounding cord. Your guide will remain in your presence, but you'll be shifting your focus to your physical body in present time.

From the center of your head, ask your personal guide what his or her purpose is in being with you. Is there any special area of assistance in which this guide specializes? You may already have gotten this information in the beginning of your meeting, but perhaps it's becoming clearer now. If you have a particular problem or project you'd like help with, ask your guide to stay with you and lend a hand.

After you're done, thank your guide and say goodbye. See your guide walking up the rainbow staircase until he or she disappears from sight. Or, if it feels better, allow this friend to stick around for a while.

As in an encounter with any flesh-and-blood friend or acquaintance, it's advisable to make proper psychic separations after you're done communicating. This can be done by feeling your heart center again and the pink-rose energy within it. Say your name to yourself, feeling your unique vibration. Say today's date to yourself, allowing yourself to return totally to present time. Feel Mother Earth saying hello to you and your body. Say hello back. Write today's date on your grounding cord. Adjust all your chakras, one at a time, back to a good balance of upper and lower (don't leave your upper chakras wide open). Finish by bending over and letting any excess energy you might have in your back, shoulders, neck, head, arms, or hands flow easily into the earth.

Meeting Other Helpers

Other spiritual helpers that might be available to you are known as masters, angels, archangels, and spiritual teachers. These evolved beings are available any time to human beings for guidance on a mass scale. This means they are helping and guiding a large portion of the planet's population. They are concerned primarily with teaching, healing, and helping advance spiritual awareness on earth.

Although masters, angels, archangels, and spiritual teachers are involved in large-scale planetary events, their work may also include special kinds of rescue missions for single individuals. Some of these highly evolved beings have never actually been on earth themselves, or were here only when the planet was being created. Others have grown through the earthly experience and have moved on to the position of helping us from the higher realms.

Devas, or angels, are another subdivision of helpers. These are helping spirits who have never been in a human body, but who have great interest in assisting humankind. Devas are closely related to the world of nature and to all nonhuman forms of life on our planet.

Children invariably have a good sense of their spiritual guidance via imaginary friends, dolls, and play animals. Often a child will communicate directly with a guide and will get help, comfort, and healing in this way. One could even consider Mickey Mouse, Snoopy, and other famous play friends as examples of masters and archangels—beings who are helping and comforting masses of children throughout the planet. Similarly, the beloved teddy bear and security blanket are examples of personal guides and helpers!

To communicate with other guides, whether they be masters, angels, archangels, spiritual teachers, helpers, or devas, prepare yourself as you did in the preceding exercise. Decide what kind of guide you feel you need to know or communicate with at this time. After having established communication with a guide, start asking questions; or allow yourself to receive impressions while going on a brief journey with your guide. Be sure to keep your body grounded and come out of meditation properly when you're finished.

Chapter Twelve

A Taste of Reading

Note: The lessons in these final chapters should be explored onJy if you have an active interest in learning how to intuitively read auras and heal. Otherwise, you may find yourself being led too deeply into an area for which you are not yet prepared. These intuitive reading and healing exercises are not intended to take the place of a school or teacher. Rather, they are meant to provide a base of experience and understanding. It's up to you to use the information wisely for yourself and for the person you're helping. It is also essential that you allow yourself to be spiritually guided in this domain of healing and helping. Be sure you've already read the previous chapters about inner teachers and personal guides.

Going into Trance

"Reading" energy is being able to perceive images, either visually, mentally, or on a feeling level, and to translate them into a meaningful message. This entire process requires a so-called trance state.

"Going into trance" is simply another term for the act of meditation. The primary purpose of trance is to transcend the right-wrong, left-right, black-white judgments humans tend to fall into. The trance state is a place of expansion and overview, a place of perceiving reality without judgment or analysis.

Depending on one's point of view, the term "going into trance" may have an impressive, mystical, or even a frightening ring to it. But all it really means is doing meditative focusing that will allow you to plug deeply into your intuitive channels. Going into trance brings you into a state of mind in which your brain produces a higher rate of alpha waves, the kind of brain activity that enables you to connect with the nonrational part of your being.

The word *trance* comes from the word transcend, which means "to go beyond." When you go into trance, you go beyond the limitations of dualistic thinking (right and wrong, black and white, left and right, etc.) to go to a place of increased understanding and neutrality.

The following step-by-step procedure will bring you into trance and will focus your awareness on information coming from your upper four chakras. You can get information through every chakra; the upper four chakras, however, are used as an intuitive unit because it's easier to be neutral from this perspective. From an upper-chakra perspective, you'll get more overview, which allows for optimum understanding and learning.

This state of mind may take more concentration than you are used to, and it may confront you with many questions. But with regular practice, it can become a comfortable part of your everyday life. Be sure to give yourself plenty of time to practice and experiment.

Before you follow the ten trance-inducing steps below, you may find it helpful to review previous workshop sections: The Center of Your Head, Grounding, Cleaning Out Your Aura, Exploding Pictures, Grounding and Owning the Room, Running Energy, and Neutrality. Here are the ten steps:

1. Come into the center of your head.

2. Ground yourself.

3. Clean out your aura and clear your visualization screen (sixth chakra) of random mental pictures by exploding them in a rose.

4. Bring in your sun.

5. Ground and "own" the room.

6. Clean out the energy channels in your feet, legs, hands, arms, and spine by visualizing a golden marble running through them.

7. Run your energy.

8. Feel yourself in a state of neutrality.

9. Adjust your chakras as you did in "Meeting Your Personal Guide," above.

10. Say your personal prayer.

Now you're ready to read!

Reading Your Own Rose

Imagine your sixth chakra (third eye) as a blank television screen that will display images when asked. Say your name inside yourself and invite a rose to appear. Look at the rose. Its openness can tell you how intuitively receptive you are. Is your rose a tiny bud? A halfway-open flower? Or is it fully open? Remember: as we grow toward increasingly refined levels, we pass continually through each stage of blossoming and decay.

Now find the sun that symbolizes your energy source, your higher self. Look at this rose in relation to the sun to determine how well connected you are with this source. Is the rose facing the sun? Does its stem have leaves or thorns? What does this mean to you? Now investigate the ground in which it's rooted. Is it deeply rooted in rich soil?

Lastly, look for any colors surrounding the rose. What do these colors tell you? Do you see any pictures, colors, or symbols anywhere else in this picture? If so, what do they suggest to you about yourself?

Thank your rose for giving you so much information. If you have passed judgment or gotten any negative feelings about yourself from this reading, simply say hello to it all and neutralize those pictures. Feel your sun essence going down into your grounding. Then come out of trance by bending and letting any excess energies run off into the earth.

The Workroom

Ask and you shall receive. This is the most important concept to keep in mind when seeking intuitive information. When reading intuitively, you'll need to actively look and ask. There are many helpful techniques to assist you in this process. One excellent way of easily obtaining intuitive information is by going to the workroom, as follows:

Go into trance, as described earlier in this chapter. Go to your sanctuary and get oriented for a while. Then imagine strolling along a pathway leading toward your "information center." This center can be a futuristic building, a mountain cave, a medieval monastery, a modern library, or whatever you envision.

Go to this information center and enter it. At the front desk, find your inner teacher or any other helper. Say hello and explain that you're looking for information concerning a certain person or subject. If it's a person, you'll need to say that person's name and date of birth (if available). The helper will tell you right away if it's appropriate at this particular time to reveal the information you're looking for.

If you have received a green light from your helper,

he or she will lead you to a room somewhere in the information center. This is the workroom, where you'll be able to find the information you are looking for. Inspect the room. Perhaps there are books on shelves. If so, read some of the titles until you come to the page you're looking for. Read it or look at the pictures, and see how the information you're receiving relates to your question.

Maybe you'll find a table in the center of the room with a crystal ball to inspect. What words, pictures, or symbols do you see? There might also be a movie, television, or computer screen on the table. If so, allow yourself to take a look. What pictures do you see? Next to these can be a computer with a printer, giving you the written information you're looking for.

If you need to know the date or time of any event, on the wall there can be a calendar and a clock. Or you may find a large globe on which certain areas are lit up to give you information about the location of certain events. There can even be an animal friend in the room conversing with you, or your helper can appear to give you the information you need.

Take your time. Look around and allow yourself to be creative and assertive in locating your information. If you're meant to have it, you'll get it. If the timing isn't right or the question is inappropriate, you won't get the information you're searching for. Universal law is as simple as this. In any case, be sure to keep the atmosphere in the room light and happy. You can "own" this room just like any other and fill it with your favorite color or colors.

Once the information starts to come to you, you'll continue to perceive as a detached observer. The next difficulty may be your own doubts as to whether the information you are getting has any useful meaning. Perhaps it'll take a while to build up your self-confidence and your belief that all of this can work. It can!

Even if you honestly believe in your information,

you may be unable to translate it into anything significant. The process takes practice and patience. You'll notice that the pictures you see or sense often become dimmer when your normal thought processes come in again—thoughts such as, "I'm doing this wrong . . . I'm not capable of getting intuitive information . . . I'm hungry . . . I've got to finish this before so-and-so comes home," and so on. Don't resist these thoughts, but don't pay any attention to them, either.

Once you've found what you're looking for, put the workroom back the way you found it and leave. Walk back along the pathway to your sanctuary. Come back to the center of your head and feel yourself sitting in your chair. Feel your sun essence and your grounding cord. Say your name to yourself in the center of your head, and then say the current date. Be yourself in present time. Open up the first three chakras and close down the upper four chakras to where they were before you started the exercise. Finally, take a deep breath, and come out of your trance by bending over.

Chapter Thirteen

Intuitively Reading Another Person

The biggest challenge in reading another person is how to determine the difference between intuitive images and your own projected fantasies. The following exercise is an idealized model of what a reader goes through to gather information. If you feel up to the challenge, it can also be used as an introduction to the experience of reading another person.

If you decide to practice this reading method, be sure NOT to program the person you are reading. Programming means telling your subject "how it is" and what choices he or she should make. Also, a reader should be especially careful not to predict future events. A fortuneteller may prove to be right about future events simply because he or she has programmed a subject with the prediction itself. Stay modest and neutral as a reader, and respect the ideas and convictions of your subject, even if you don't agree. Perhaps hearing some of your views can eventually open up new possibilities for the subject.

To practice as a novice, you need to feel very comfortable with your subject. Conversely, your subject should feel open minded about your explorations. While reading, always stay in tune with your friend on a heart level and frequently ask for feedback. Check to see whether the subject recognizes what you are seeing or sensing.

If you're not sure whether the pictures you perceive are yours or the subject's, you can explode them in a rose. If the pictures come back after a series of explosions, it's very likely they really are reflections of your subject's reality. This is a very effective method of distinguishing clairvoyant pictures from personal pictures. If you still are not sure after having exploded pictures, you can always discuss it with the subject and see what feedback you get. If the subject reacts emotionally to those pictures, you have probably hit on some worthwhile information.

To begin reading another person, first go into trance. Then, saying your prayer at the end of preparation, ask for help from your spiritual guides according to your own needs and feelings. Follow the ten steps described in the section Going into Trance in the previous chapter, then add the following steps:

11. Increase your neutrality by symbolically visualizing a rose or several roses between yourself and the person you're reading. These roses will absorb and neutralize any energy coming toward you. Check to see where your psychic boundaries are and make sure you're feeling secure in your psychic space.

12. Stay within your psychic space, and remain focused on the sixth chakra. Check your analyzer, and turn it down if necessary. Remember not to go into the psychic space of the other person!

13. Be aware of chakra cording. During a reading, there should be no cords at all between yourself and your subject. You need to be as neutral and detached as possible.

14. Give special attention to grounding and owning the room. Owning the room doesn't mean leaving the center of your head. It merely means that you are making the room completely safe and comfortable.

As you'll probably notice, it takes a special presence of mind to remember all these points. Fortunately, if you practice regularly, you can move from thinking into an intuitive plane of awareness quite easily.

The Reading

The person you are reading should be sitting with feet flat on the floor, hands apart, and eyes open. The two of you should be in chairs about four feet apart and facing each other: Ask the subject to say his or her name several times. This makes the person "more present" and makes his or her vibration more apparent. Do you notice any colors or qualities coming up from the sound of the subject's voice?

Now focus on your sixth-chakra screen and ask yourself to see a rose symbol reflecting specific qualities about your subject. Tell your subject what you see and ask for comments.

One of your hands can be held with your palm facing the subject as a way of receiving more information through your creative hookups. Try both hands to discover which one feels like the receiving hand.

With your eyes closed, ask to see the person's aura. Look around the body, not forgetting the legs and feet. Is the person grounded? Get a sense of this by inspecting the subject's grounding cord.

What colors do you see in the grounding cord and the aura? What do these colors mean to you? Do you see any pictures or symbols in the aura or physical body? What are they trying to say? Ask to receive answers in a language that the subject can understand. Discuss what you're seeing with the subject and ask for feedback.

If you see any pictures that remind you of yourself or make you feel emotionally involved, stop! Before proceeding, put those matching pictures in a neutralizing rose, not forgetting to bring the sun symbol into your body and aura afterward. This procedure is of vital importance while doing any intuitive work. It's an ongoing process that needs to be performed almost continuously during any reading.

When you are exploding matching pictures, it's a good idea to make sure you still have good psychic separations between yourself and the subject. Check specifically for chakra cords that might make you reactive and subjective instead of neutral and detached. Although it may feel good, even a heart cord can keep you from being neutral enough for a proper reading. After cleaning out any cords, check to make sure your lower chakras have remained relatively closed and the upper ones open.

Now focus on the person's chakras, one by one, and ask to get a picture, according to your own symbolism, of what each one looks like. What colors do you see? Is the chakra open or closed? Is it blocked with any dark colors? Do you see any pictures or symbols there? What do these things have to tell you? Discuss what you're seeing with the subject and ask for feedback. Remember to be tactful when relating any negative information. Doing this is not always easy, but remember that your guides can help you!

The reading can proceed from here in any way you or the subject finds appropriate. If necessary, go to the workroom and search for important information relevant to any of the subject's questions. Remember, you'll only be admitted to the workroom if given a green light to do so. Certain kinds of information from the workroom are available only when a person is ready to hear it.

Throughout the reading, make sure you and the subject are in your own psychic spaces. Remember to breathe, ground, run energy, stay neutral, explode matching pictures, own the room, and so on. Keep checking for chakra cords and neutralizing them.

As the reading draws to a close, be sure to visualize returning any energy you might have taken on from your subject. Imagine it going back into the sun above the person's head. Make sure they are completely in their own space, asking them to focus on the center of their head if necessary.

Clean out your own aura, explode any remaining matching pictures, and bring in your sun symbol afterward. Say your name to yourself and feel yourself totally focused in present time. Thank your guides for helping you, and put them outside your aura if you feel it's necessary. Adjust your chakras for everyday life, bend over, then slowly sit up.

Chapter Fourteen

Intuitively Healing Another Person

Most of the information in this workshop concerns itself with healing in one form or another. All the exercises you have done so far are aimed at increasing awareness of your energy patterns through your power to visualize and/or sense intuitively. Hopefully, this has contributed to your increasing sense of "coming home" and of being more the person you really want to be. All real healing is a homecoming, because it's based on a reunion with your highest creative essence.

All reading contains elements of healing, and vice versa. The similarities have to do with recognition and validation of the subject, which a successful reading can provide. So how does one go about healing someone intuitively?

Begin just as if you were preparing to give a reading. Systematically work on the steps described in Chapter Thirteen of this workshop, Intuitively Reading Another Person. In addition, open up your hand chakras some more and concentrate on the energy flowing through your creative hookups. This allows your heart and hand chakras to be a cooperative "healing unit." Healing someone does not mean you go into sympathy with them. Make sure you're neutral, even on a heart level. It's highly recommended to say your own prayer before healing and to ask help directly from your healing guide or guides.

What are you actually going to be healing? It can be any-thing from a bad mood to a terminal illness, because healing is the act of helping a person get in closer contact with his or her highest creative essence. You, as a healer, are helping others on an energy level to "find their way home."

The Healing

After you have prepared yourself, ask the person being healed to say their first and last name. This will help you come into contact with the subject's unique vibration. Say hello to this name silently inside yourself until you get some kind of reaction from the name in return. This might be a hello, but it might also be a squeak of surprise or even a response such as "Get out of here!" Whatever the reac-tion, keep saying hello to the name until you get the feeling you're communicating on the same energy level.

This "hello" ritual is very basic yet extremely im-portant. It's a way of tuning into the subject's condition and sensing how open the person is to receiving help. Saying hello can set the stage for validation of the subject's par-ticular situation, no matter what it is. It shows a respectful attitude toward the subject's own problem solving. Many times, this validation and acceptance of a person and their higher self is the most powerful aspect of any healing.

Something important to consider when starting a healing is the amount of humor available to the subject at any given time. Humor allows stagnant energies to flow again, which is what healing is all about. Problems and ail-ments can only settle into the psyche or physical body when energies are blocked and don't flow properly anymore.

After the subject's grounding cord has been estab-lished, either sense or look with your mind's eye at how much humor is sitting inside that umbilical cord with Moth-er Earth. If it appears to be lacking in humor; add some yourself by visualizing funny things, or tickling the grounding cord and hearing it laugh inside yourself, or by filling it up with little pink bubbles or tiny ringing bells.

Now communicate with the subject's particular kind of humor by asking her to say her name again and seeing what comes up in your imagination. When working with humor, remember that there are endless ways to have fun. Some people might benefit the most from quiet, introverted joy, while others might get the most out of a blatant laughing fit. Be open to all possibilities!

The next step is to connect the subject to the earth by increasing his or her grounding. This grounding can be seen as a connection with the person's physical source of being. All elements in our bodies originate from the earth. Bodies rebuild and sustain themselves by partaking of the earth's sustenance. Connect the subject with a grounding cord by standing behind them while they are sitting. Put your hands on their shoulders and imagine all tension is draining out of their body and flowing easily into the earth.

Visualize the subject as having a strong grounding cord, or add to the grounding any healing picture that the person already has. Make sure you aren't projecting your own ideas about grounding. Ask the subject's name again, and communicate with that energy to receive more pictures about how he or she would like to be connected to the earth. What kind of material should the grounding cord be made of? How big does it need to be? What color or colors does it want to be? In what way would it like to be connected to the center of the earth? Silently ask many questions of this kind. Tune into the subject's name, then visualize these new changes happening.

The visualizations you project into the subject's grounding serve as a point of crystallization for their own way of connecting with the earth. How receptive the subject will be to your suggestions depends on the character of the subject.

Visualizing is not a test of will; it's merely a way of suggesting changes on an energy level. Children and sensitive adults usually respond positively to pictures of transformation projected into their psychic territory. If you don't get much information about what kind of grounding the subject needs, ask the center of the earth to send up an appropriate cord and imagine it happening.

Suggesting changes by projecting positive pictures into someone's psychic space is basic in the intuitive healing process. Another important aspect of intuitive healing is the ability to channel healing energies through your creative hookups. By using your intuitive unit (the fourth, fifth, sixth, and seventh chakras, with the sixth chakra as a focal point) and your healing unit (the fourth chakra combined with creative hookups via hands and arms), you are in optimum form to give a healing. Once your healing unit has been cleaned out by imagining you are running golden marbles up and down your arms (from palms to heart chakra), or that you are filling the hands and arms up with golden light, you are ready to be a channel for healing energies.

The energies you channel are either part of the unique energy system of the subject, or are part of the larger energy system of the earth and cosmos. You should never use your own personal energy to heal somebody. Personal energy (one's own highest creative essence—one's own sun) has a unique vibration that only fits the body and psyche to which it belongs. Giving your personal energy to somebody else will drain you and will not be of any help in the long run.

The ability of a healer to channel universal healing force or the subject's own highest creative essence leads us down the path of true healing. There are endless healing guides available to all of us at every moment of the day, ready to help and comfort humankind. Humans are like riddle books with the answers hidden in the back of the book.

All our problems have answers somewhere inside us, and the big challenge is how to find them.

How do you channel a person's highest creative essence? An excellent way of doing this is by perceiving or visualizing the subject's brilliant golden sun above their head and bringing this sun energy, via the healing unit, toward the subject's body. By beginning to use your healing unit, you can visualize your hand chakras working something like magnifying glasses: they can magnify energies just as sun rays can become concentrated through the focus of a lens. In helping the person to ground, you can imagine their unique sun essence being channeled through your hands, which are resting on your subject's shoulders. This sun essence will move all the way down to the first chakra area, where the grounding begins.

Either during or after the sun healing, universal cosmic and/or earth energies can be given in this same way. Simply ask for it to happen. Your and the subject's guides are waiting to be of service.

You also need to feel free to move your hands around, inside, and outside of the subject's aura, according to what spontaneously occurs. Or, take a look through your sixth-chakra visualization screen and "know" through your seventh-chakra radio receiver whether there are certain areas in the subject's aura that need healing. You can perceive these needy spots as dark, empty, sad, or simply needing a hello. Place your hands above or directly on these spots, tune into the person's name, and ask the person's energy what color is needed here.

Gold is an excellent color to begin with because of its energy-raising and purifying qualities. Other good colors for stimulating energy are pink (affinity and love), orange (creative force), and green (harmony, balance, and growth). Good colors for quieting and soothing are green, light blue to blue (peacefulness and certainty), and lavender, light violet, and light purple (psychic-spiritual atunement). Allow the needy part of the subject to tell you what colors it can most benefit from in the moment.

Now imagine your healing unit bringing in the color or colors to the area that needs healing. See it being bathed in color. Make massaging and cleansing movements in the air around the area you're working on. To neutralize old energies, shake your hands off occasionally, as if you were shaking off water.

Check the person's chakra system and see which chakras might need healing. Do you sense any parts or organs of the physical body that need healing? If so, perhaps a "laying on of hands" would be appropriate. Always stay in touch with the subject's energy. If you don't know whether you've brought in enough energy, ask for a red or a green light to tell you: red for stop the healing, it's enough now; green for continue the healing, the subject may receive more. A good way to end a healing session is by reconnecting the subject with their sun essence, the vibration of the immortal self. Imagine, again, a powerful sun shining brightly above the subject and visualize it bringing light, health, happiness, and freedom into their body and psychic space. Do this either by visualizing it or by directing the energies with your hands.

Ask the subject to bend over and stretch. Meanwhile, finish the healing by making psychic separations: Sit down and think of at least three neutral physical differences between yourself and the subject—for instance, "I have red hair and hers is blonde," or "He has white pants and mine are blue," etc.

Feel yourself, your own face, your own hands, your own heart. Say your name to yourself and imagine any personal energy that might have leaked out of your system corning back to your third chakra. Return any personal energy you might have taken to the subject's solar plexus. A playful yet powerful way to return personal energies is to imagine yourself being, for instance, an orange and the subject a banana. See all the energy of the orange being returned to you and the energies of the banana being returned to the subject.

Thank your healing guides for their help, and make psychic separations, if necessary. Check the cords you might have created and disconnect them. Adjust the openness of your chakras for everyday life. Neutralize any matching pictures. Feel your own unique sun essence and your own way of connecting with the earth. Imagine the energy of the room you've been working in to be bright and clear, and any heavy or difficult energies easily draining away through the grounding cord of the room. Come out of trance by bending over and having a good stretch.

World Healing

You can send healing thought-forms to the entire planet, just as you can to one single person. Imagine yourself in a spaceship looking down at Mother Earth. See her being surrounded and penetrated by radiant healing light that will always endure. Say a few words of comfort and encouragement. Return to the earth in your spaceship and go back to your sanctuary. Feel how safe and comforting it is to be connected to the earth with your grounding cord. Thank Mother Earth for all she does for you. Realize how important your visualizations, thought-forms, and projections are in creating the present and future matrix of our earth's reality.

About the Author

LINDA KEEN is an American healer, author, and teacher of metaphysics, as well as a professional musician and former school counselor. She began her metaphysical practice in 1978 in the Netherlands after discovering her aptitude for using her intuition to help others. Providing support to clients looking for significant answers to questions concerning a soul's purpose in everyday life, Linda unwittingly pioneered an entirely new method of training within the Dutch self-help community. Her book *Intuitieve Ontwikkeling* (*Intuitive Development*), published in 1985 (*Intuition Magic*, 2nd English edition, Keen Press), quickly became a best seller and is in its 19th printing in Holland. In both the Dutch language and in English, the book remains a landmark resource for those seeking encouragement in this field. The most striking realization Linda had in the course of her work was how each and every human being has full access to his or her own elaborate body of spiritual information—if only they have the interest required to seek and find it. This access is one of the lesser-known and/or acknowledged gifts of the remarkable human psyche. As many now know, the gift of the imagination is truly the most powerful tool we humans possess in determining our ability to "be still and know," and it remains the primary source of all our self-healing.

Visit Linda Keen's website at www.keenintuition.com.

Made in the USA
San Bernardino, CA
19 January 2020